HEINEMANN WORK-BASED LEARNING

NVQ/SVQ & Technical Certificate

Level 2

EG LLANDRILLO

Cleaning

Diane Canwell • David Pope • Tricia Rivers
Caroline Roberts • Ruth Whaites

www.pearsonschoolsandfe.co.uk

✓ Free online support
✓ Useful weblinks
✓ 24 hour online ordering

0845 630 44 44

Heinemann

Part of Pearson

Heinemann is an imprint of Pearson Education Limited, a company incorporated in England and Wales, having its registered office at Edinburgh Gate, Harlow, Essex, CM20 2JE. Registered company number: 872828

www.pearsonschoolsandfecolleges.co.uk

Heinemann is a registered trademark of Pearson Education Limited

Text © Pearson Education Limited 2009

First published 2009

12 11 10 09

10 9 8 7 6 5 4 3 2 1

British Library Cataloguing in Publication Data

A catalogue record for this book is available from the British Library

ISBN 978 0 435501 20 4

Copyright notice

Designed by Jerry Udall
Typeset by Jerry Udall
Original illustrations © Pearson Education, 2009
Illustrated by Julian Mosedale and Sean @ KJA Artists
Cover design by Pearson Education
Cover photo/illustration © Istockphoto
Printed in Spain by Graficas Estella

Acknowledgements

The authors and publisher would like to thank the following individuals and organisations for permission to reproduce material:

JohnsonDiversey (pp.18-19); www.safetyshop.com (pp.24-25); figure on p.177 reproduced under the terms of the Click Use licence, with thanks to the Health and Safety Executive.

The authors and publisher would like to thank the following individuals and organisations for permission to reproduce photographs:

© Pearson Education Ltd, p3; © Pearson Education Ltd/Stuart Cox, p8, p9, p11, p23, p32, p62, p63, p84; © Tommy (Louth)/Alamy, p86; © Paul Thompson Images/Alamy, p88; © Pearson Education Ltd/Stuart Cox, p90, p91, p92; © Renee Morris/Alamy, p97; © Pearson Education Ltd. Jules Selmes, p106; © Pearson Education Ltd/Stuart Cox, p107; p112; © F1online digitale Bildagentur GmbH/Alamy, p.125; © VIEW Pictures Ltd/Alamy, p125; © Biju/Alamy, p125; © Iconpix/Alamy, p125; © Archimage/Alamy, p125; © Pearson Education Ltd/Stuart Cox, p158, p159; © Pearson Education Ltd/Stuart Cox, p162; © Coollife/Alamy, p169; © DK Images, p185 (both images); © Pearson Education Ltd/Jules Selmes, p189

Every effort has been made to contact copyright holders of material reproduced in this book. Any omissions will be rectified in subsequent printings if notice is given to the publishers.

The websites used in this book were correct and up-to-date at the time of publication. It is essential for tutors to preview each website before using it in class so as to ensure that the URL is still accurate, relevant and appropriate. We suggest that tutors bookmark useful websites and consider enabling students to access them through the school/college intranet.

Contents

Contents

Level 2 Cleaning Qualifications

As a representative of the cleaning industry and your employer you are responsible for the cleanliness and appearance of the environment in which you work. You play a vital role in maintaining health and safety standards. By undertaking training, you are making a commitment to raising standards throughout the industry and promoting cleaning as a profession. The cleaning *NVQs* and the *Certificate in Cleaning Principles* (the Technical Certificate) are designed to promote professionalism, uphold and improve standards in the cleaning industry.

The *Certificate in Cleaning Principles* covers the knowledge and skills required by cleaning staff. It is an industry and nationally recognised qualification. There are three mandatory units which all candidates must take, and then you can choose at least one optional unit to match the field of cleaning in which you are working. The certificate shows that you have a level of knowledge and skill that means you are ready to work as a cleaner.

The NVQ provides an industry and nationally recognised qualification. It confirms that the skills and knowledge gained from the *Certificate in Cleaning Principles* are being competently and consistently practised and demonstrated to meet the National Occupational Standards.

A combination of these two qualifications along with several Key Skills form a structured programme of training called an Apprenticeship. However, the cleaning NVQs and the *Certificate in Cleaning Principles* are both also available as standalone qualifications.

NVQs

What is an NVQ?

An NVQ assesses a person's technical competence to perform a job. The assessment is continual but you will only be assessed when you are competent at a task. NVQs are divided into units. In order to pass a unit you need to fulfil various requirements:

- **What you must do** – details the actions you must undertake to pass the unit.

- **What you must cover** – details the range of situations, tasks and commodities that you need to demonstrate you can cover.

- **What you must know** – the statements of knowledge you must show that you understand.

How do I gain an NVQ?

The flowchart below summarises the process of gaining an NVQ.

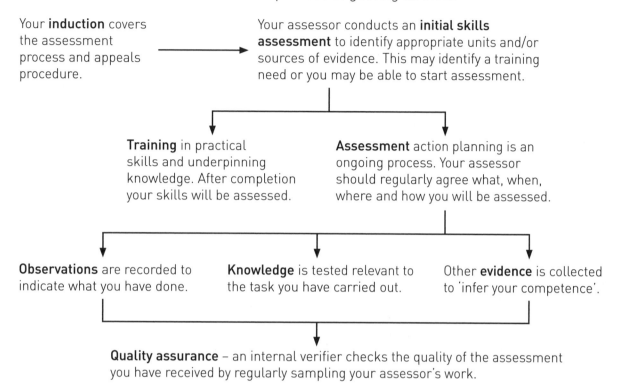

Your **induction** covers the assessment process and appeals procedure.

Your assessor conducts an **initial skills assessment** to identify appropriate units and/or sources of evidence. This may identify a training need or you may be able to start assessment.

Training in practical skills and underpinning knowledge. After completion your skills will be assessed.

Assessment action planning is an ongoing process. Your assessor should regularly agree what, when, where and how you will be assessed.

Observations are recorded to indicate what you have done.

Knowledge is tested relevant to the task you have carried out.

Other **evidence** is collected to 'infer your competence'.

Quality assurance – an internal verifier checks the quality of the assessment you have received by regularly sampling your assessor's work.

Your portfolio

All evidence should be placed into your portfolio and will need to be referenced to the NVQ standards. You may be given a paper logbook showing these standards. There are different styles of logbooks depending upon which awarding body you are registered with. Alternatively you may be using an e-portfolio.

Apprenticeships

What is an Apprenticeship?

Apprenticeships offer an opportunity to train and gain national and employer recognised qualifications specific to a chosen career, while working in the industry. Apprentices in your organisation may be existing staff or external applicants who wish to pursue a career in the cleaning industry. The Apprenticeship consists of a number of qualifications which make up an Apprenticeship framework. The Cleaning Apprenticeship Framework consists of:

- **Knowledge-based element**

    Certificate in Cleaning Principles

- **Competence-based element**

    NVQ Level 2 in Cleaning & Support Services

- **Key/Essential Skills**

    Application of Number Level 1
    Communications Level 1

All Apprentices are also required to complete an Employment Rights and Responsibilities document which forms part of the Apprenticeship induction process

How do I gain an Apprenticeship?

The Apprenticeship Framework states the requirements for this qualification. How an Apprenticeship is gained can be very flexible and is dependent on the Apprentice's job. For example, large employers may run Apprenticeships alongside existing training programmes. The training for the *Certificate in Cleaning Principles* could be delivered in workshops at the employer's premises or by day-release or evening classes with a training provider. The NVQ will be assessed within a real working situation.

Mapping grid

Book chapter	NVQ / SVQ Level 2 Cleaning and Support Services	Technical Certificate Level 2 Cleaning Principles
Chapter 1: Health, safety and security	201.1 204.1, 204.2	202.1, 202.2, 202.3
Chapter 2: Communication	202.1	203.1, 203.2
Chapter 3: Working in teams and developing yourself	203.1, 203.2, 204.3	203.3
Chapter 4: Dealing with routine and non-routine waste	207.1, 207.2 216.1, 216.2	201.1, 201.2
Chapter 5: Cleaning internal surfaces and areas	205.1, 205.2	209.1, 209.2, 209.3 (part)
Chapter 6: Cleaning washrooms	208.1, 208.2	209.1, 209.2, 209.3 (part)
Chapter 7: Cleaning high risk areas	209.1, 209.2	208.1, 208.2, 208.3, 208.4
Chapter 8: Cleaning food areas	211.1, 211.2	206.1, 206.2, 206.3

Health, safety and security

What you will learn:

- Health and safety responsibilities
- Risk assessment
- Health and safety regulations
- Safety data sheets
- Other regulations
- Equality and diversity

Health and safety responsibilities

British health and safety law is based on the Health and Safety at Work etc. Act 1974. According to this Act both employers and employees have duties that they need to carry out to ensure health and safety in the workplace.

Your employer needs to:

- carry out risk assessments (see pages 4–6)

- provide equipment and materials, tools, machinery and appliances that are safe to use and are properly maintained by regular checking

- prepare and communicate, to all their staff, a health and safety policy

- ensure safe systems of work and adequate supervision

- provide employees with the training and supervision necessary to ensure their health and safety while at work

- make arrangements for the safe use, handling, storage and transport of all equipment, appliances, tools and products

- provide the necessary personal protective equipment (PPE, see page 8) and safety devices free of charge

- ensure that employees follow the procedures described in the health and safety policy

- provide adequate facilities, e.g. clean, well-lit toilets.

As an employee you need to:

- work safely by obeying the safety rules set out in your company's health and safety policy

- take care of your own safety as well as the safety of others who may be affected by what you do or do not do

- correctly store materials and equipment so that they are not a danger to others

- make sure you do not interfere with or misuse anything that your company has provided to protect your and others' health and safety

- report immediately any health and safety hazards you may notice

- be aware of the emergency procedures, including fire evacuation. You need to take part in fire and emergency training and make sure you are aware of where equipment required in the case of a fire is stored and where the emergency exits are

- co-operate with your employer to improve the company's safety management system.

Health and safety responsibilities

DEFINITIONS

Procedures

Procedures are set ways of doing things. These are usually written down, either by a company or by a customer.

Safety management system

A safety management system is the formal process of assessing and making improvements to safety in the workplace.

Emergency procedures

Emergency procedures tell you what to do if a potentially dangerous event such as a fire or a security alert occurs.

Health and safety policies and procedures are written down to ensure that the employer and employee act responsibly in accordance with the law.

An employer who has five or more employees is legally obliged to have a health and safety policy. Employers with fewer than five employees do not have to have a health and safety policy but it is recommended to have one.

It is important you know the procedures to follow in the event of a fire.

TASK

☐ Write down how your behaviour in the workplace can affect your and your colleagues' health and safety.

_____

_____

_____

☐ Read your employer's health and safety policy and write down what is expected from you by your employer.

_____

_____

_____

Risk assessment

As will be seen from the health and safety legislation outlined in this chapter, employers have an important duty to carry out **risk assessments**. To fully understand what is meant by risk assessment, it is useful to understand some of the terms used in health and safety.

DEFINITIONS

A hazard

A hazard is something that has the potential to cause harm. For example, toilet cleaner in a sealed bottle has the potential to cause harm but if it is left in the sealed bottle and stored correctly it presents very little risk.

Risk

Risk is the chance of a given harm occurring in specific circumstances. For example, an open container of toilet cleaner left on a window sill in a public toilet.

Risk assessment

This is a procedure by means of which the hazards present while doing a task are identified and the chances (risks) of that hazard occurring are estimated, taking into account any precautions that are already being taken.

TASK

☐ How should cleaning chemicals be stored to ensure that the risks they present are minimised?

_____

_____

Most risk assessment systems are based on the five-step approach suggested by the Health and Safety Executive (HSE). The five steps are:

1 Identify those **hazards** that could reasonably be expected to result in significant harm in the workplace, e.g. chemicals, slipping, tripping hazards, electrical equipment.

2 Identify who may be harmed – several people doing similar work or who may be affected by that work, e.g. other staff, visitors.

3 Identify if more needs to be done to control the **risk** – for the hazards found, do the precautions already being taken meet the standards set by legal requirement?

Risk assessment

4   Comply with recognised **industry standards**.

5   Represent **good practice** and reduce risk as far as reasonably practicable.

If an employer has fewer than five employees there is no requirement to record the risk assessment. However, employers of more than five employees must record the important findings of their assessment. They should also inform their employees of their findings.

If, after step 3, there are still some hazards remaining, the person undertaking the risk assessment has to decide if the remaining risks are high, medium or low.

If the risks remain high or medium it has to be decided what extra precautions are required to reduce the risks as far as reasonably practicable.

Industry standards

Industry standards are standards that are agreed throughout an industry as being the correct method or way of operating in that industry.

Good practice

Good practice is not just about meeting the industry standards but improving on them.

TASK

☐   Where are the risk assessments affecting your job kept?

_____

☐   When was the last time they were reviewed?

_____

☐   Explain why it is important that you understand the importance of any risk control measures.

_____

_____

_____

Risk assessment

Once a risk assessment has been carried out the employer will have identified:

- the extent of any risk
- how to, wherever possible, reduce the risk to an acceptable level (this can be done by perhaps changing the way a job is carried out or fitting safety equipment to machinery such as a trip switch)
- the PPE that is required while carrying out a particular task
- the safe systems of work to control risks.

A safe system of work sounds very complicated. In some cases such as working within a confined space they may well be. However, often it may be as simple as using colour-coded equipment to avoid **cross-contamination** between areas, that is using different coloured cloths to clean toilets and damp-wipe dining room tables, for example.

TASK

Using colour-coded cloths is a safe system of work. Briefly describe why it should be used and the risks that it helps to reduce.

_____

_____

_____

TASK

Identify five safe systems of work that you use while carrying out your tasks and why it is important to follow them.

1 _____

2 _____

3 _____

4 _____

5 _____

Health and safety regulations

The main **regulations** that apply to the cleaning and support services industry are described briefly below. You should be aware that these regulations are amended from time to time. So it is important that you keep your knowledge up to date. The **Health and Safety Executive** (HSE) website is a good source of up-to-date information.

DEFINITIONS

Regulations

Regulations are rules that must be followed by law by all employers to avoid risks in the workplace that the government has identified. The rules describe the specific actions the government requires employers, and in some cases employees, to take to avoid risks.

Health and Safety Executive

The Health and Safety Executive is the body responsible for ensuring that both employers and employees follow health and safety at work laws and regulations.

Competent

A competent person is someone who is trained and qualified to identify existing and potential hazards. They also may have the authority to take action immediately if a safety hazard is identified.

Management of Health and Safety at Work Regulations 1999

These regulations require employers to carry out risk assessments, plan the necessary procedures to improve safety, ensure that the procedures are carried out by appointing **competent** people to the task, and arrange for appropriate information and training for staff.

These regulations also require employers to set up emergency procedures to deal with such things as a fire or an explosion. You should be aware of your company's emergency procedures in case the worst happens.

TASK

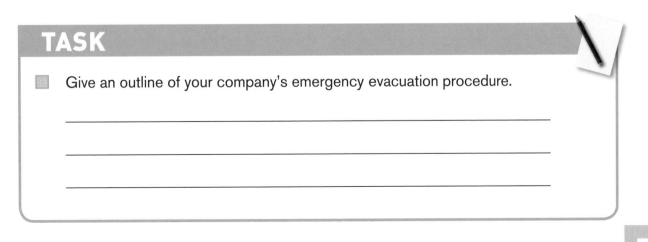

☐ Give an outline of your company's emergency evacuation procedure.

_____

_____

_____

Unfortunately, the risk of a terrorist attack is always present. So it is important that you are always on the look out for unusual things such as suspicious packages or bags lying around or people acting in a suspicious manner.

If you come across something that you feel is unusual, it is important that you know the correct procedure to deal with it. This means knowing whom to report to so that the occurrence can be investigated and the correct action taken to deal with it quickly and effectively. You should be able to find this information in your company's and/or your customer's emergency procedures policy.

You should always report unattended bags or suspicious packages.

Personal Protective Equipment (PPE) at Work Regulations 1999

The main requirements of these regulations are:

- The employer should supply **PPE** to all employees working wherever there are risks to health and safety that cannot be controlled in other ways.

- All employees should use the PPE that they have been supplied with.

- The employer should ensure the PPE is used. If an employee is not doing so, they can use the company's **disciplinary procedures** to make them do so.

Health and safety regulations

DEFINITIONS

PPE

PPE is equipment which may include clothing that should be used when there are risks to your own health and safety while working. For example, when working with chemicals or to avoid cross-contamination.

Disciplinary procedures

Disciplinary procedures are a formal process used by an employer to change an employee's behaviour or to ensure that the employee adheres to the employer's rules and/or policies.

Cross-contamination

Cross-contamination is the pollution of one area with dirt or germs carried from another area or yourself.

TASK

☐ Describe the PPE you have been supplied with.

_____

_____

☐ What is the importance of wearing the correct PPE?

_____

_____

The correct footwear should protect and support your feet.

Your employer will supply PPE to protect you from the hazards associated with the job you are carrying out. But you also have a responsibility to ensure that when at work your own clothes or other personal items that you are wearing do not put your or others' health at risk.

An example of this is footwear. Most employers will state that footwear worn by their cleaning staff should fully enclose the toes and support the heel. This is because if something falls on your foot, your toes have some protection. Also, without support for the heel, your footwear will slip around and could cause a slip or trip accident.

TASK

▢ What is your company's dress and personal hygiene policy while carrying out your job role?

_____

_____

_____

▢ What is your company's policy on wearing jewellery while at work?

_____

▢ Why is it important that you adhere to the policy?

_____

_____

Make sure your personal presentation while in the workplace meets your company's expectation. In this way you will meet your employer's health and safety requirements. You will also present a professional image to your customer that reflects well on both you and your company.

DEFINITION

Personal hygiene

Personal hygiene is the way in which you look after yourself and make sure that you are clean and tidy.

Electricity at Work Regulations 1989

These regulations require employers to assess the risk of working with electrical equipment. This is commonly called PAT testing, which stands for Portable Appliance Testing. Portable appliances can include a vacuum cleaner or a scrubber dryer. Once the risk has been assessed then the information can be used to reduce unacceptable risk.

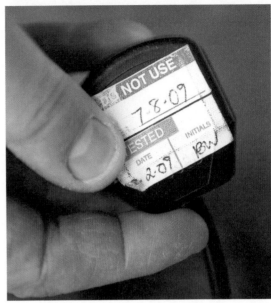

The frequency and type of testing of electrical equipment will depend on the type of equipment, how often it is used and the environment in which it is used.

Electrical equipment should be tested regularly according to the law.

As an employee, it is your duty to always check before using any portable electrical appliance for safety in the way you have been trained.

Provision and Use of Work Equipment Regulations 1998 (PUWER)

These regulations require that equipment provided for use at work is:

- suitable for the intended use
- safe for use and maintained in a safe condition. Some equipment will need to be inspected at regular intervals to ensure it is safe to use
- used only by people who have received adequate information, instruction and training in its use
- accompanied by suitable safety measures, e.g. protective devices, warnings.

These regulations do not list any specific responsibilities for employees. However, your duties as described in the Health and Safety Act 1974 do apply. This means following both the manufacturer's instructions and any instructions given to you by your employer.

TASK

☐ Why should you only use equipment in accordance with the manufacturer's instructions?

_____

_____

_____

☐ What may happen if you do not follow the instructions?

_____

_____

_____

TASK

☐ What checks would you carry out on a piece of electrical equipment before using it?

_____

_____

☐ Why are these checks important?

_____

_____

☐ If you come across a piece of faulty equipment, what procedure do you follow to ensure that no-one else uses it before it is repaired?

_____

_____

_____

Manual Handling Operations Regulations 1992

This regulation requires that employers should avoid their employees having to carry out hazardous manual handling (see below), as far as they reasonably can.

For this, your company would have assessed the risk of injury from hazardous manual handling which can be avoided. It would also have procedures in place to reduce the risk of injury from hazardous manual handling, as far as they reasonably can.

As an employee, your duty is to always make sure you:

- follow the appropriate **systems of work** laid down by your company for employees' safety
- make proper use of the equipment provided for your safety
- co-operate with your employer on health and safety matters
- inform the responsible person if you identify hazardous handling activities
- take care to ensure that your activities do not put others at risk.

> **DEFINITION**
>
> **Systems of work**
>
> Systems of work are procedures and practices put in place by employers to ensure that the health and safety of workers is not at risk while they are carrying out a function in an appropriate way.

Manual lifting and handling

Before trying to lift any object, you should ensure it is not too heavy or awkward for one person to lift. If it is, you must ask for help.

If the object is to be lifted then the lifter should:

- stand with the feet apart

- if lifting from a low level, always bend the knees, with minimal bending of the back

- use a hook grip rather than keeping fingers straight

- keep loads close to the body

- not jerk or twist when lifting.

Figure 1.1. Lifting can cause injury if not done properly.

Figure 1.2. Always start with a good posture.

Control of Substances Hazardous to Health Regulations (COSHH) 2002

Manufacturers spend a lot of time testing their products to find the safest and most economical and efficient ways of using their products. If their instructions are not followed the effectiveness of their product may be reduced.

COSHH requires employers to:

- assess the risk of using a product

- decide what precautions employees should take while using the product

- prevent or adequately control exposure to the product

- ensure **control measures** are used and maintained

- monitor exposure

- carry out appropriate health surveillance (checks) – where a risk assessment has shown this to be necessary

- prepare plans and procedures to deal with incidents (accidents) while using the product and emergencies

- ensure employees are properly informed, trained and supervised while using the product.

> **DEFINITION**
>
> **Control measures**
>
> Control measures are actions or procedures that are used to reduce health and safety risks while using certain products.

TASK

☐ Why is it important to follow the manufacturer's instructions when using cleaning chemicals?

_____

_____

_____

☐ If the manufacturer's instructions state that the dilution rate for a cleaning chemical is 1:5, what does this mean?

_____

_____

Reporting of Injuries, Disease and Dangerous Occurrence Regulations 1995 (RIDDOR)

RIDDOR requires employers to report the following incidents within a set period of time:

- In the case of death or major injury of an employee or self-employed person working on the premises, the **enforcing authority** must be notified without delay (e.g. by telephone). Within 10 days, this initial notification must be followed up with a completed Accident Report Form.

- An injury which is not major but results in the injured person (employee, self-employed person working on the premises) being away from work or unable to do the full range of their normal duties for more than three days (including any days they wouldn't normally be expected to work such as week-ends, rest days or holidays)

not counting the day of the injury itself should be reported to the enforcing authority with an Accident Report Form within 10 days.

- If a doctor notifies the employer that an employee is suffering from a reportable work-related disease, a completed Disease Report Form must be sent to the enforcing authority.

- Dangerous occurrences – if something happens which does not result in a reportable injury, but which could have done so, it may be a dangerous occurrence and must be reported immediately to the enforcing authority.

Your employer is required by the law to report injuries and dangerous occurrences. However, it is in both your employer's and your own interest to ensure that accidents do not happen.

Under the Health and Safety Act 1974, as an employee, you have the responsibility to report health and safety hazards immediately.

DEFINITION

Enforcing authority

The enforcing authority is usually the environmental health department of a local authority.

TASK

☐ Briefly describe your company's procedure for the reporting of accidents.

_____

_____

_____

Safety data sheets

Many cleaning products are harmful if used incorrectly. For this reason, a safety data sheet is produced by the supplier of the cleaning product. Your company should receive a copy of the safety data sheet (see pages 18–19) before you use the product.

The safety data sheet should contain the following information:

- name of the substance
- name, address and telephone number (including an emergency number) of the supplier
- composition/information on the ingredients of the product
- physical and chemical properties of the product
- hazard identification (what risks can occur)
- first aid measures
- fire-fighting measures
- accidental release measures (what to do if spillage occurs)
- personal protection required when using the product
- stability and reactivity (is it likely to explode or catch fire?)
- toxicological information (is it poisonous?)
- ecological information (will it harm the environment?)
- disposal considerations (does it need to be disposed of in a special way?)
- transport information (does it need to be carried in a special way?)
- regulatory information (the regulations that apply to this product).

There is a lot of important information in a safety data sheet which will affect how you store and use cleaning chemicals.

Your employer should have:

- carried out a risk assessment on the chemical
- given you full training on the use of the chemical and the precautions you should take when working with this chemical including the safe and secure storage of cleaning materials.
- Overleaf, as an example, an MSDS for the product 'Taski Sani Acid W3F', a heavy duty washroom descaler from JohnsonDiversey.

SAFETY DATA SHEET

1. IDENTIFICATION OF THE SUBSTANCE / PREPARATION AND OF THE COMPANY / UNDERTAKING

JohnsonDiversey   JohnsonDiversey UK Limited
Weston Favell Centre Northampton NN3 8PD Tel 01604 405311 Fax 01604 406809 Emergency Call 0800 052 0185

Clearance Code	TASKI SANI ACID W3f	Product Code
R61410	Professional cleaning/maintenance product for building care	MSDS5057

TO :

2. COMPOSITION / INFORMATION ON INGREDIENTS

CAS No	EINECS No			
7664-38-2	231-633-2	Phosphoric acid (WEL)	C: R34	(>30%)
69011-36-5	polymer	Alkyl alcohol ethoxylate	Xn: R22-41	(<5%)

Ingredients according to EC 648/2004:
More than 30% : Phosphates
Less than 5%   : Nonionic surfactants
Perfumes, Benzotriazole

Full text of R-phrases is given in section 16.

3. HAZARDS IDENTIFICATION

Corrosive - causes burns.
This product contains a material with an WEL published in HSE document EH40.

4. FIRST AID MEASURES

Eyes : Rinse immediately with copious amounts of water, holding the eyelids open and obtain immediate medical attention.

Inhalation : Remove from source of exposure. Seek medical advice if effects persist.

Skin : Flush the contaminated area with running water, remove contaminated clothing and wash before re-use. If irritation persists or there is any sign of tissue damage seek medical advice.

Ingestion : Remove product from mouth, give the casualty a small quantity of water to drink and obtain immediate medical attention. Do not induce vomiting.

5. FIRE FIGHTING MEASURES

NON FLAMMABLE - In the event of a fire due to other causes the product is compatible with water, foam, carbon dioxide and dry powder extinguishers. Firefighters should wear self contained breathing apparatus and suitable protective clothing including gloves and eye/face protection.

6. ACCIDENTAL RELEASE MEASURES

Wear suitable protective clothing including gloves and eye/face protection. Hose away with plenty of water diluting to at least 1% w/v (10 g/litre) unless this would contaminate a water course or vegetation, in which case either collect, dilute as earlier and pour down wastewater drain (foul sewer) or absorb onto dry sand or similar material and dispose of to a licensed waste management company.

7. HANDLING & STORAGE

Avoid contact with skin, eyes and clothing. Wear suitable gloves and eye/face protection. Do not mix with any other chemicals other than as advised by your JohnsonDiversey representative.

Store upright in original containers in a cool place. Keep tightly closed.

8. EXPOSURE CONTROL / PERSONAL PROTECTION

Hand : Use gloves resistant to Phosphoric acid.

Eyes : When handling neat product wear eye/face protection to EN 166.

Skin : Wear normal workware overalls or coat.

Respiration : Personal protection is not normally required unless a risk assessment indicates the need for it.

Date: 25/10/2005   Revision Number: -   Page: 1 of 2

Figure 1.3. Safety data sheets are produced by the supplier or producer of a cleaning agent.

Safety data sheets

Product Name	TASKI SANI ACID W3f	Product Code	MSDS5057

WEL :	Orthophosphoric Acid, (Phosphoric Acid)	ref. HSE publication EH40
	W.E.L. 2 mg/cu.m 15 min ref time	

9. PHYSICAL & CHEMICAL PROPERTIES

Appearance :	Clear colourless liquid	Odour :	Slightly perfumed
pH :	<2.0	Solubility :	Fully miscible with water
Density :	1.21 g/cm³		

10. STABILITY & REACTIVITY

Keep away from alkali's. Keep away from aluminium, tin, zinc and their alloys. Provided the product is stored in accordance with the approved guidelines there are no known hazardous decomposition products.

11. TOXICOLOGICAL INFORMATION

Eyes :	Corrosive - causes burns
Skin :	Corrosive - causes burns
Inhalation :	Severe irritant - Inhalation of spray mists will cause irritation of the respiratory tract.
Ingestion :	Corrosive - Strong caustic effect on mouth and throat and danger of perforation to oesophagus and stomach.

12. ECOLOGICAL INFORMATION

When used for its intended purpose this product should not cause adverse effects in the environment.

13. DISPOSAL CONSIDERATIONS

This product does not contain any prescribed substance under the Environmental Protection Act (Prescribed Processes and Substances) Regulations 1991 but is classified as special waste under the Control of Substances (Special Waste) Regulations 1996. For small quantities wear suitable gloves and eye/face protection. Dilute with water to at least 1% w/v (10 g/litre) and pour down a wastewater drain (foul sewer). Rinse out containers at least twice and recycle if facilities exist or dispose of as commercial waste. For larger quantities contact a licensed waste management company.

European waste catalogue 20 01 14   acids

14. TRANSPORT INFORMATION

EEC Regulation :	C, CORROSIVE, Phosphoric Acid, Solution, UN1805, Hazchem 2R
IMDG/UN :	Phosphoric Acid, Solution, UN1805, Class 8, PG III
RID/ADR :	Class 8, Item 17(c)
ICAO/IATA :	Passenger Aircraft: 819, Y819
	Cargo Aircraft: 821

15. REGULATORY INFORMATION

Hazard symbol :	C, CORROSIVE, Contains Phosphoric Acid	
Risk phrases :	R34	Causes burns
Safety phrases :	S26	In case of contact with eyes, rinse immediately with plenty of water and seek medical advice.
	S28	After contact with skin, wash immediately with plenty of water.
	S36/37/39	Wear suitable protective clothing, gloves and eye/face protection.
	S45	In case of accident or if you feel unwell, seek medical advice immediately (show the label where possible).

This product contains a material with an WEL published in HSE document EH40.

16. OTHER INFORMATION

Handle and apply only as recommended, for full information see product information sheet.

Internal Reference:-   MSDS5057-03(25-Aug-2005), FABNX05W30 (19-Jul-2005)

Text of risk phrases associated with ingredients listed in section 2.

R22	Harmful if swallowed
R34	Causes burns.
R41	Risk of serious damage to eyes.

Chapter 1

Health, safety and security

Other regulations

There are other regulations, which as an employee you should know about. Even if employee responsibility is not specified within these rules and regulations (called legislation) you must remember that your responsibilities under the Health and Safety at Work etc. Act 1974 will still apply. You also have the duty to report any safety hazards, use equipment and supplies properly and follow any training and instructions given to you by your supervisor or other responsible person.

TASK

▢ From your job description identify your responsibilities for health and safety in your workplace.

_____

_____

_____

If you do not work at your company's site, for example if you work for a cleaning contractor, you may not ever go to your employer's offices. However, you will still be required to follow your employer's policies and procedures. You will also be expected to follow your employer's customers' policies and procedures. These may be different from your employer's.

TASK

▢ Why is it important that you follow the security requirements of your company's customer?

_____

_____

_____

▢ Identify where your company's customer's health and safety policies may differ from your company's in the use of PPE, specifically footwear.

_____

_____

Other regulations

- The Health and Safety Information for Employees Regulations 1989 – this requires employers to inform employees about what they are required to know about health and safety and to display appropriate posters.

- Employers Liability (Compulsory Insurance) Act 1969 – this requires employers to take out insurance against accident and ill health for their employees.

- Work at Height Regulations 2005 – this applies to all work at height from which there is a risk of fall causing personal injury. In such cases the employer has the responsibility to control the work. This means that the employer has to carry out risk assessments to ensure risk is minimised. They also have to ensure that any safety precautions that are identified in the risk assessment as being required are put in place.

- Confined Spaces Regulations 1997 – this applies where a risk assessment identifies that there is a risk of serious injury from work in confined spaces. In such cases the employer has the responsibility to ensure the safety (as far as is reasonable) of the employees working within a confined space.

- The Workplace (Health, Safety and Welfare) Regulations 1992 – these require employers to ensure that sanitary and washing facilities are clean, ventilated and well lit.

- Chemicals (Hazard Information and Packaging for Supply) Regulations 2002 – this regulation applies to manufacturers of chemicals. The manufacturer has responsibility to supply certain information concerning their products. They have to decide what kind of hazards the chemical has and explain the hazard by assigning a simple description to it (known as the risk phrase). This process is known as classification. Once the chemical/product has been classified the manufacturer then has to tell its customers:

  - about the hazard

  - how the chemical/product may be used safely, for example with safety data sheets.

Health, safety and security

Other regulations

TASK

Name at least four policies produced by your company to cover its legal obligations for health and safety. Where are the policies kept and when was the last time they were reviewed?

Policy	Location	Last reviewed

The Health and Safety at Work etc. Act 1974 requires employees to report health and safety hazards immediately. The process for doing this may be different in different companies and work sites.

TASK

☐ Who is the person responsible for health and safety within your company?

_____

☐ Who is the person responsible for health and safety at your workplace?

_____

☐ What is the procedure for reporting hazards in your company or workplace?

_____

☐ Identify five hazards which may occur in the workplace:

1 _____

2 _____

3 _____

4 _____

5 _____

Other regulations

If you come across a hazard or risk in your workplace and you are able to deal with it without endangering yourself or anyone else you should do so. Following this you must report it.

If you cannot deal with the hazard or risk yourself, you must follow your company's procedures for reporting it. Usually your first contact would be with your line manager or supervisor, who will then contact the other people outlined in the procedure.

Before reporting the hazard or risk you must take all reasonable steps to ensure that the hazard or risk is isolated and clearly visible. You can do this by placing warning signs or by isolating an area.

It is vital you alert people to potential hazards by placing warning signs.

TASK

☐ When reporting a hazard or risk what information should you give?

_____

_____

☐ Why is it important that the information is clear and concise in relation to the risk?

_____

_____

Symbols

It is important that you understand the symbols that appear on the packaging of cleaning materials. This is to ensure that you store the chemicals correctly and wear the appropriate PPE when using the chemical.

DEFINITION

Ambient temperature
Ambient temperature is the temperature of the air around us.

23

	Explosive.	This symbol denotes a substance which may explode under a flame or if it is subjected to shocks or friction.
EXPLOSIVE	Oxidising.	This symbol denotes a substance which releases a lot of heat while it reacts with other substances, particularly flammable substances.
OXIDIZING	Extremely flammable.	This symbol denotes a liquid that would boil at body temperature and would catch fire if exposed to a flame.
EXTREMELY FLAMMABLE	Toxic.	This symbol denotes a highly hazardous substance.
TOXIC	Very toxic.	This symbol is used to label a substance which, if it is inhaled or swallowed or if it enters the skin, may involve extremely serious, acute (immediate) or chronic (longer-term) health risks and even death.
VERY TOXIC	Harmful.	This symbol should appear on the label of a substance which, if it is inhaled or swallowed or if it enters the skin, may involve some health risks.
HARMFUL		

IRRITANT	Irritant.	The same symbol but with the word 'irritant ' is meant for a non-corrosive substance which, through immediate, prolonged or repeated contact with the skin or mucous membrane (the lining of your mouth and other body organs such as your foodpipe and stomach), can cause inflammation (redness, swelling, pain or rise in temperature).
HIGHLY FLAMMABLE	Highly flammable.	This symbol denotes a substance which: o may become hot and finally catch fire in contact with air at **ambient temperature** o is a solid and may readily catch fire after brief contact with the source of ignition and which continues to burn or to be consumed after removal of the source of ignition o is a gas and burns in air at normal pressure o in contact with water or damp air releases highly flammable gases in dangerous quantities o is a liquid that would catch fire with slight warning (that is, it may change from liquid to gas) and exposure to a flame.
CORROSIVE	Corrosive.	This symbol is found on the label of a substance which may destroy living tissues on contact with them. Severe burns on the skin might result from splashes of such substances on the body.
Dangerous for the environment	Dangerous for the environment.	This symbol refers to a substance which if released untreated may cause damage to the environment.

TASK

Look at the warning signs on the labels of the chemicals you use regularly.

Identify from the warning signs on the packaging what type of hazard the chemicals are designated. Also check what PPE the manufacturer recommends should be worn when using the chemical.

Chemical	Hazard	Recommended PPE

Lone working

Some people working in the cleaning industry work on sites at times when the buildings are empty apart from themselves. Although there are no specific health and safety regulations covering lone working it is covered by the Health and Safety at Work etc. Act 1974 and the Management of Health and Safety Regulation 1999. Your employer should have a policy and procedures in place that you should follow if you are a lone worker.

Equality and diversity

The cleaning industry employs men and women from many countries, backgrounds and cultures. Your workmates may differ from you in many ways such as:

- gender

- religion

- race

- colour

- sexual orientation

- physical ability.

It is important that employers and employees treat everyone in a fair and equal way. You must make sure that your behaviour does not discriminate against anyone. This means you should treat everyone with equal respect, however different they are. If every member of the team works hard at this, the team will be strengthened.

There are Equal Opportunities laws to make sure that individuals and groups of people do not suffer from harassment or discrimination because they are different.

Your employer should have a policy for this. It will be called either an 'Equal Opportunities Policy' or an 'Equality and Diversity Policy'. It is important that you understand this policy and follow it.

DEFINITIONS

Equality

Equality means everyone has the right to an equal level of respect and opportunity.

Diversity

Diversity means valuing the differences between people.

Harassment

Harrassment means being bullied or tormented, or being made to worry about things unnecessarily.

Discrimination

Discrimination means treating an individual or a group differently from everyone else, usually unfairly.

Health, safety and security

Knowledge test

1 **Which of the following statements is a definition of a hazard?**

   a. Something that has the potential to cause harm.

   b. Something that has the potential to cause an accident.

   c. Something that has the potential to be dangerous.

   d. Something that has the potential to injure you.

2 **Which one of the following statements defines a risk?**

   a. A chance of a given loss occurring in specific circumstances.

   b. The likelihood of a given loss occurring in specific circumstances.

   c. When a loss may occur if the risk is not dealt with correctly.

   d. When a loss will occur if the risk is not dealt with correctly.

3 **The Health and Safety at Work etc. Act 1974 placed responsibilities on:**

   a. the employer.

   b. the employee.

   c. both employer and employee.

   d. the employer and monitoring agencies.

4 **The Health and Safety at Work etc. Act 1974 requires that you:**

   a. work safely and obey rules.

   b. work quickly and efficiently.

   c. work to ensure the job is completed.

   d. work to your supervisor's instructions.

5 **If you came across a damaged electrical socket within the workplace what action would you take?**

   a. Find another electrical socket that wasn't damaged.

   b. Report it to your supervisor or maintenance department.

   c. Ensure no-one else can use it and report it to the appropriate person.

   d. Warn colleagues not to use it until it is repaired.

6 **Prior to using a cleaning chemical it is important to know what risks the chemical presents to those using it. Where may the correct information be found within the workplace?**

   a. Chemical packaging and chemical safety data sheet.

   b. Asking an experienced supervisor or colleague.

   c. The Internet.

   d. The sales literature for the cleaning chemical.

7 **Why is it important to remain alert to the presence of hazards in the whole workplace?**

   a. To ensure that you are safe when working.

   b. To ensure it is a pleasant working environment.

   c. To ensure a safe environment for all.

   d. To ensure that you get the job done quickly.

8 **Why is it important to deal with or report risks?**

   a. It is a legal requirement.

   b. It shows you know your job.

   c. Your employer would expect it.

   d. To avoid injury to anyone.

Knowledge test

9   **Why are responsibilities for health and safety usually given in a job description?**

a. So the employer can avoid legal action.

b. So you know what is expected of you.

c. It is a legal requirement.

d. So there is someone to blame.

10   **When cleaning public areas it is important that you:**

a. look clean and smart.

b. display warning signs.

c. appear friendly and approachable.

d. are helpful if asked a question.

11   **If you identify a potential hazard, why should you report it to the appropriate person?**

a. So that you are no longer responsible.

b. To make a good impression.

c. So the hazard may be dealt with.

d. Customer expects it.

12   **In a company, who would be the most appropriate person to speak to concerning a very difficult health and safety problem?**

a. Union representative.

b. Line manager.

c. Health and Safety Officer.

d. Work colleague.

13   **Identify one risk from the list below that you should NOT deal with:**

a. Spillage of water on a vinyl floor.

b. An unlabelled container of cleaning fluid.

c. A damaged electrical cable on a vacuum cleaner.

d. A wrongly diluted cleaning chemical.

14   **Colour-coded equipment is used to:**

a. identify whose equipment it is.

b. avoid cross-contamination.

c. identify where the equipment is to be used.

d. avoid the expense of disposable equipment.

15   **Why is it important to follow the manufacturer's instructions when using cleaning chemicals?**

a. Efficiency, economy and health and safety.

b. Efficiency, economy, health and safety and staff training.

c. Staff training, health and safety, efficiency.

d. Efficiency, economy and staff training.

16   **Why is it important that you comply with your company's rules on personal presentation?**

a. To ensure your health and safety.

b. To avoid disciplinary action.

c. You are representing your company.

d. Customer expectation.

Health, safety and security

17 **What is the most important reason to behave sensibly while at your workplace?**

a. Customer expectation.

b. To avoid disciplinary action.

c. To avoid accidents.

d. Aid team work.

18 **Where would you find information on the environmental impact of the cleaning chemical you use?**

a. Asking an experienced line manager.

b. Risk assessment sheets.

c. The chemical's packaging and safety data sheet.

d. The Internet.

19 **If you find a suspicious package, what should you do immediately?**

a. Open it.

b. Run away.

c. Inform your supervisor or security.

d. Forget about it.

20 **RIDDOR stands for which of the following?**

a. Reporting of Injuries, Disease and Dangerous Occurrence Regulations.

b. Replicating of Injuries, Disease and Dangerous Occurrence Regulations.

c. Reporting of Injuries, Disinfectant and Dangerous Occurrence Regulations.

d. Reporting of Injustice, Disease and Dangerous Occurrence Regulations.

Chapter 2

Communication

What you will learn:

Why communication is important

Communication allows us to pass on ideas, information and suggestions to each other. Communication is a two-way process: one person starts the communication, and another person receives the communication. We need to make sure that the person receiving the communication has understood what the sender is saying. This requires **feedback**.

How we communicate

Speaking face-to-face or on the telephone, writing notes or messages and sending emails are all examples of communication. Sometimes we communicate without even knowing it. A smile, a wink, a hand movement and even the way we stand are all ways in which we communicate.

TASK

☐ Think about the ways in which you communicate every day at work. In how many different ways do you communicate?

_____

_____

_____

In a normal working day, you may communicate in a number of ways. Sometimes your communication will be simple. At other times it will be more complicated. Also, some types of communication are better than others in certain situations. For example, people might find it hard to explain something very complicated by just talking about it. You might need to write it down.

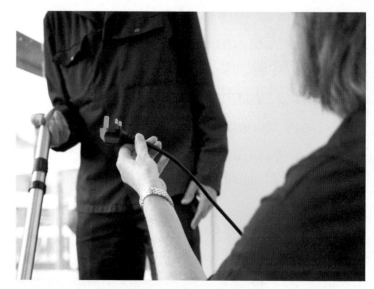

Think about what is the best way to explain a task to someone.

Communication is vital. You will need information to help you carry out your job. You will also need to be updated if there are any changes to what is expected of you.

Keeping in touch when you work alone

There are some jobs that you will be doing on your own. You will not have others to work with or daily contact with a supervisor or manager. But you still need to keep in touch with them and find out about the procedures you need to follow. Sometimes there will be regular opportunities to meet up or report in. This could be face-to-face or over the telephone. These are your chances to highlight any problems you are experiencing. Your supervisor or colleague could also use these opportunities to let you know about any changes required of you.

Communicating in teams

Teams work well when team members communicate well. By communicating, they can share ideas and information. So communicating makes the team more efficient and work better. This is because everyone knows what is expected of them and what has been done or what still needs to be done.

TASK

☐ Are there procedures in your workplace to ensure you keep in touch?
Explain what they are.

_____

_____

_____

The importance of your behaviour and attitude

What you say

What you say and how you say it is important. It is not just important because people will form an opinion about you after listening to you. They may also form an opinion about the company you work for.

When you speak, it is not only your choice of words that matters, but also how you actually say those words. This is even more important than how helpful, polite or well mannered you are. Remember that it is very easy for people to get the wrong impression. So you always need to think before you speak.

TASK

Think about how you communicate in your workplace. How do you communicate with the following people?

☐ Supervisor:

_____

_____

☐ Client:

_____

_____

☐ Team member:

_____

_____

About your attitude

Simple things can say a lot about your **attitude**. When you are speaking to someone face-to-face, always try to:

- look them in the eye, but don't stare
- pay attention to what they are saying
- show them you understand by smiling or nodding your head
- be polite
- be helpful
- make the other person feel valued
- always end the conversation with a smile and say goodbye.

When you are speaking to someone on the telephone this can be more difficult, but you can still:

- answer the telephone as quickly as possible
- answer with 'good morning', 'good afternoon' or 'good evening'
- tell them your name
- answer with the hand you do not write with, as you may have to take a message
- try to have a paper and pen ready by the telephone
- confirm that you understand
- assure them that you will do what they are asking you to do
- if necessary, repeat what they have said to show that you have understood
- do not forget to pass on any messages you are given.

You and your company

Remember that you represent your company. Many people will not see anyone else from your company apart from you. What you say and your attitude will give them an impression about your company. So your behaviour always needs to be:

- positive

- clear

- helpful

- polite.

TASK

☐ Does your company have set ways (also called protocols) of dealing with customers?

_____

☐ Does everyone in the company have to address the customer in a certain way?

_____

_____

_____

☐ What sort of image of itself does your company want to give to the customers?

_____

_____

_____

The importance of a positive image

Your company has to keep its customers. Without customers it will make no money. And without money the company will not be able to pay its staff.

You need to give a positive image of your company because:

- it helps create and maintain a good relationship with customers

- it shows that your company cares about its customers

- it shows that your company's staff are well trained and helpful

- it might mean that customers would recommend your company to others

- it encourages customers to communicate with you and your company.

Figure 2.1. A positive image is important because you represent your company.

The information you might need

Most work can be routine. Once you have been shown what to do, it will just be a matter of getting on with it. But things do change and so might your work. So you need to make sure you have all the information you need to carry out your job. Above all, if there are changes, you must know who can tell you about them so that your information is up to date (see page 42).

Therefore you must have all relevant information and it must be up to date. Also, you have to be sure that you understand it.

There may be times when no one is available to give you information or help. It will be up to you to decide whether to carry on with a task or to wait. Putting off doing something is not always possible, so you might need to make your own mind up about the best way to tackle everything.

TASK

Why would the following changes affect the way in which you work?

- [ ] Changes in health and safety regulations

  _____

  _____

- [ ] Introduction of new cleaning agents

  _____

  _____

- [ ] A new team member

  _____

  _____

Finding the right information

It is rare for jobs to stay the same for very long. Changes are always taking place. **Procedures** and ways of doing things are always being updated. Often the problem is finding out where the right information that you need is located.

DEFINITIONS

Procedures

Procedures are set ways of doing things. These are usually written down, either by a company or by a customer.

Staff handbook

A staff handbook is a file of instructions on ways of doing things. A company usually wants all staff to follow its own handbook or set of rules.

Here are some examples of different sources of information:

- your manager or supervisor

- your customers

- other members of your team

- your **staff handbook**.

In some cases you will have to use your own skills and knowledge to make a decision about something. As you become more experienced at your job the quicker and easier it becomes to make that decision. In most cases you will know the best way to deal with something and will not need to ask others for information to help you.

Verbal information

Sometimes, to help you carry out your job, you will need advice, help or instructions from someone else. You need to be as clear as you possibly can when you ask questions. This will help you carry out your job to the best of your ability. The person you ask a question of may not be able to give you an answer straight away. They may have to talk to someone else first. Knowing whom to ask is your first step to gaining the right information.

Advantages of verbal information:

● it is quick

● you can ask if you do not understand

● you can ask questions.

Disadvantages of verbal information:

● you need to speak clearly

● not ideal if the information is complicated

● you do not have a record of what was said.

Written information

Sometimes if certain things have changed about your work you will receive your new instructions in writing. Or you may have to ask for it to be put in writing so that it is clear and you can keep it to refer to later. Some companies produce **newsletters**. They send these out to all staff so everyone knows the latest information. Other companies send a **memorandum**, which is another way of providing written information.

Advantages of written information:

● a record is created, which you can re-read when needed

● it can be copied and given to others

● you can use pictures to make things clearer.

Disadvantages of written information:

● it needs to be accurate

● it can take longer to create

● it can become lost.

DEFINITIONS

Newsletters

Newsletters are written by different members of staff in a company and sent to all staff. They contain news and information that everyone in the company needs to know.

Memorandum

A memorandum is like a note or a letter. Unlike the newsletter, a memorandum is not sent to all the staff in a company. It is sent to some members of staff with information to help them with particular areas of their work.

Checking information is up to date

It is a lot easier to check whether information is up to date if it is written down. This is because it will probably have a date. Checking whether the information that you receive verbally is up to date or not is more difficult.

You will probably need to check that the person who is giving you the information is working from the latest available information. This is because there is a danger that they may tell you something that is no longer true. If this happens, you could end up doing something you do not need to do, or you may do something in a way that is wrong. This is particularly important as your work involves using chemicals, and your health and safety is a priority.

Making sure you understand

If you are given written information, it might be hard to check immediately with the writer anything that you do not understand in it. But they might have asked you to contact them to confirm your understanding. This is your opportunity to clear up anything you have not understood or you think you may have misunderstood.

When you are given verbal information make sure that you fully understand what the other person is saying to you before the conversation finishes. Remember that communication is a two-way process.

Types of communication

Verbal communication

As you can see in the diagram below, **verbal communication** can take place face-to-face or over the telephone. Verbal communication is of different types. It also happens in a variety of different situations. Different types of verbal communication may be used in particular situations.

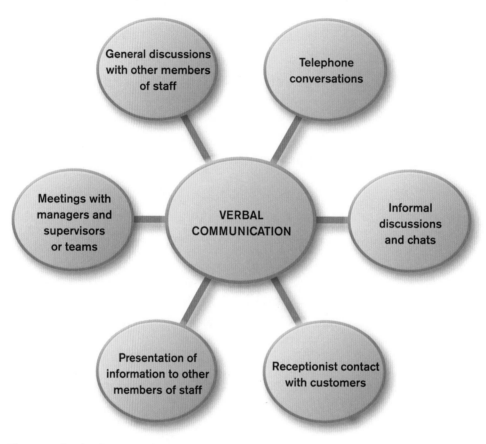

General discussions with other members of staff

Telephone conversations

Meetings with managers and supervisors or teams

VERBAL COMMUNICATION

Informal discussions and chats

Presentation of information to other members of staff

Receptionist contact with customers

Figure 2.2. These methods of communication are verbal in nature.

Some methods of verbal communication are formal. For example, when people discuss things in a meeting or are being given a presentation. In formal situations, someone usually takes notes (called minutes), so there might be a chance in the future that you will see these notes. Notes can help you remember what was said and what had been agreed.

However, most methods of verbal communication are informal: either face-to-face or on the telephone. Rumours and gossip are also examples of informal communication. But you should never rely on these to give you accurate information.

DEFINITION

Verbal communication

Verbal communication is the passing on of information by directly speaking to someone, either in person or on the telephone.

Types of communication

Written communication

Just like verbal communication, there are plenty of different ways of using written communication. Sometimes written communication might just be a scribbled note. But at other times it may be longer and more complicated. The diagram shows you some typical types of written communication:

Figure 2.3. These methods of communication are written.

Written communication can also be either formal or informal. Emails, notes and messages tend to be informal. Most of the others, such as letters and notes, are more formal. Written information is all designed to pass on information or instructions. You will be expected to respond to most written communications you receive, even if just to confirm that you have received and understood them.

Having things in writing means you can refer back to them whenever you need to. For example, you can check whether you are following any new procedures or instructions correctly. Or you can check the deadline date of a task or the name of the person you wish to contact if you need to ask something.

DEFINITIONS

Written communication

Written communication is the passing on of information by the written word.

Body language

Body language is communication that takes place between people from the movements of their body and facial expressions.

TASK

Look at the following list and tick which methods of communication are written or verbal:

☐ Cleaning agent instructions ☐ Telephone conversation with employer

☐ Note from your supervisor ☐ Team meeting with your co-workers

Non-verbal communication

Non-verbal communication is all about:

- facial expressions
- gestures
- eye contact
- posture
- personal appearance.

Non-verbal communication is also known as **body language**. It can support what you are saying. So you need to be aware that your body language will be giving off non-verbal signals to the person you are talking to. Even little things you do while you are talking can either support what you are saying or send mixed messages to the other person.

Types of communication

TASK

Look at the list below and tick the examples of non-verbal communication:

☐ Smile   ☐ Telephone conversation   ☐ Frown

☐ Work schedule   ☐ Eye contact

There are several types of non-verbal communication:

- Facial expressions, such as smiling, moving the eyebrows or widening the eyes are all things that happen without our being aware of doing it.

- Gestures are like a sign language, such as nodding in agreement or using your hands to help describe something.

- Even the way you sit, and position your hands, feet and shoulders all can influence the other person's impression of you when they are listening to you talk.

- Eye contact is important, but this should not be misunderstood as simply staring.

Figure 2.4. You can communicate with people without saying a word!

Why it is important to communicate clearly

Clear communication means that fewer mistakes and misunderstandings happen. You would expect anyone communicating with you to make sure that they tell you what you need to know and ensure you understand. When you are communicating with other people this is your responsibility. You need to find the best way to communicate with them. You also have to check that they have understood you.

Communication takes place in plenty of different situations. Sometimes you are rushed. Sometimes you are tired. Sometimes you might not know enough about something to communicate it well. At other times, the other person may simply not understand, no matter how hard you try.

How to communicate clearly:

- you need to make yourself clear
- avoid using slang
- know when to speak
- do not interrupt
- know what questions to ask
- use your body language carefully.

Needs of different people

How you say it, when you say it and how complicated you make it will depend on who you are communicating with:

- English may not be your or someone else's first language. So this might be something to consider
- some people need complicated information to be broken down for them
- some people do not need to be told everything but just what is relevant to them
- some people will simply not be interested because it does not affect them.

Understanding the need for providing enough information

For someone to be able to act on information or follow instructions you need to make sure that they have all the information they need. There is no point in telling people part of the information as this will only confuse them. People might request information to:

- make a decision

- know what to do next

- know how to do something

- know where to find something

- know whom else to ask.

Sharing information

Making sure that everyone who needs to know something is given that information makes everyone's life easier.

It is important that everyone is kept up to date with the latest information. This avoids mistakes being made, people doing work that does not need to be done, or doing something the wrong way.

People need information to do their jobs. You can share or swap information at meetings, or when you see someone at work. If information is not shared then all kinds of problems will occur. It also makes working as a member of a team very difficult, as some people will have up-to-date information and others will not know why things are being done differently.

Responding positively

You may be very busy and may have very little time to spare. But there are times when customers or the public may ask you questions or have queries that they want answering. It may be a simple question or problem that you can help with. You should always be as positive as possible and provide them with the information they need. If you cannot answer the question yourself then you should direct them to someone who can. Remember that you represent your company and this is all part of creating a positive impression.

It is also important to be aware of your limit of authority (see page 52). Although you can often deal directly with queries or requests for help, such as a spillage on the floor, there are times when you need to pass the questions to your supervisor. You should do this particularly when health and safety regulations and procedures could be compromised.

Figure 2.5. If you don't have the information you must refer the question to someone else.

Dealing with questions or queries

If someone asks you to solve a problem for them you should:

- concentrate and give them your full attention
- listen to what they are saying
- show you are listening by nodding or smiling and looking at them
- ask any questions you have that might help you understand their query
- give them a positive answer if you can
- apologise if you cannot answer their question yourself
- direct them to someone else if you cannot answer their question.

TASK

◻ Give an example of questions you may be asked by a member of the public or a client.

_____

◻ How often can you answer them yourself?

_____

◻ Do you know whom to pass the questions to if you cannot answer them yourself?

_____

_____

Equipment/Surfaces to be cleaned	Frequency of cleaning (daily/wkly/mthly)	Materials to be used	Method of cleaning	Precautions needed	Cleaning to be carried out by	Checks to be done by
Toilet bowl & seat	Twice daily	Bleach and anti-bacterial	Apply & use brush and disposable wipes	Gloves and open window	JS	DC
Cistern	Weekly	Anti-bacterial	Disposable wipes	None	JS	DC
Hand basin	Daily	All purpose	Cloth and abrasive pad	None	JS	DC
Floor	Daily	Floor cleaner	Sweep, then mop	Wet floor hazard sign	JS	DC
Door and fittings	Weekly	Anti-bacterial	Disposable wipes	None	JS	DC
Toilet roll holder	Weekly	Anti-bacterial	Disposable wipes	None	JS	DC

Figure 2.6. Work schedules need to be completed and returned.

Acknowledging incoming information

Your company or the place in which you work may have procedures that are set down about how you are expected to acknowledge incoming information. You may need to:

- contact someone and confirm that you have received the information

- produce something, such as a time sheet or work schedule

- do something and then confirm it is done

- check something and then acknowledge you have received the information.

Different companies have different ways of doing things. It is important that you know how your company expects you to acknowledge incoming information.

Responding to incoming information

Your company or workplace will expect you to read any information that you have been sent to update you on your job. If the information is about new instructions, you must carry them out. Your supervisor or manager will check to see that you have done this. They will know that you have received the information because you would have acknowledged it. You should not ignore it.

Information needing to be recorded

You may be expected to record all sorts of different information. It will depend on your job. Some common examples are:

- the hours that you have worked

- the areas that you are responsible for

- your cleaning routine for those areas

- any **consumables** that you may have used up

- any materials or equipment that you are responsible for

- any problems that you may have had with materials or equipment.

> **DEFINITION**
>
> **Consumables**
>
> Any cleaning products that you use and have to replace from time to time are called consumables.

TASK

☐ What types of information do you have to record?

_____

_____

☐ Does your company or workplace provide you with forms or documents that you have to complete?

_____

☐ Where do they have to be sent and how often do you have to send them?

_____

Procedures for recording information

Each company or workplace will have its own procedures for recording information. Some companies will provide forms to complete and you will be expected to complete these and return them by a particular date. You may have to put dates in these forms and sign them.

Your supervisor or manager may have explained the purpose of the forms and the procedures to follow. You should be checking to see you are doing the right thing. You can do this by asking your supervisor or manager, or checking a staff handbook if you have one.

Chapter 2

Communication

What does authorised mean?

Authorised means someone in your company or workplace is entitled to see particular information. They will expect the information to be sent to them, as they will need it to do their own job.

These people are likely to be more senior members of staff in the company or workplace. They may not be your supervisor or manager. But in most cases these are the people who are authorised to receive information from you.

Exactly what information and to whom that information should be sent will be part of the procedures of the company or the workplace. You should not send information or show information to people who are not authorised to see it.

Why do they need the information?

Here are some examples of different types of information. Next to each is given the people who are authorised to receive this information, and why they need that information:

- Timesheets – the person dealing with your wages will need these so they can work out your pay.

- Equipment information – a service engineer would need this information so they can routinely check equipment for health and safety purposes.

- Consumables used – whoever re-supplies you with cleaning products needs to know what you have and what you need to re-order.

TASK

☐ Who are the authorised people who can ask you for particular information?

_____

☐ What do they use this information for and how often do you have to send it?

_____

Ways of passing on information

Remember that the two main ways of communicating with others are verbal and written. You may have to pass information on to authorised people in either way. Simple pieces of information can be handled by verbal communication, where you are simply answering a question or confirming something. This is an informal way of passing on information.

Your company or workplace may insist on a more formal way of passing on information. They may have designed forms or documents, which need to be completed, dated and signed by you. It is easier for them to check written communication and to file it away so they can look at it later.

Following procedures

Your company or workplace probably has a mixture of formal and informal ways of passing information on to authorised people. It will depend how complicated and involved the information is and how often it has to be passed on. Often it is a matter of getting into the habit of filling in a form. When the form is complete or due to be sent you must do this. Sometimes the information will need to be with a person by a particular day.

There are many different ways that information is passed on in the workplace. Some of them are formal and others are informal:

Formal:

- meetings

- memoranda

- documents

- presentations

- updates or newsletters

- one-to-one meetings with supervisors or managers.

Informal:

- conversations

- emails

- notes.

Chapter 2

Communication

53

What problems might occur?

Sometimes you will have information that you need to pass on. But you may run into problems while doing this. Here are some typical examples:

- You might not know who you need to tell.
- You might only have part of the information and need more of it to provide a clear answer.
- You might not be able to contact a particular person.
- You might not have the right form to complete.
- You might have been asked to provide some information, but you do not have it.

How can this affect others?

Other people may be relying on you to provide them with information. They might not be able to do their job without it. They may make a mistake or do something wrong because they do not have this vital information.

Cooperating with other people

Most jobs rely on good teamwork. Cooperation means being helpful and working together to get jobs done. To cooperate properly and avoid problems when you have to pass on information you should:

- be concerned about the needs of the other team members
- be friendly and sociable
- try to avoid arguments
- follow the rules
- respect others' points of view
- keep the others up to date
- trust one another.

How to come up with a solution

If you have a problem in passing on information to someone then there always has to be another way of getting it to them. For example, if you normally have to complete a form but you have run out of blank copies of the form, you might have to contact someone by telephone or visit them in person to pass on the information.

Sometimes the normal way of passing on information would be to do it verbally. But the situation might be too complicated and it might be better to write it down.

There might also be someone else who is authorised to receive that information. This is often the case if the person you normally send the information to is on holiday or on sick leave. Someone else will then be responsible while they are away.

Taking the right action

Think about how you might have dealt with a similar problem before. You could use the same solution.

It also depends on how urgent the information is and how vital that information is to the other person. If in doubt always contact someone authorised to answer your questions. Ask for their advice.

> ### TASK
>
> ▢ If your manager or supervisor is on holiday who takes over from them?
>
> _____
>
> ▢ Are these persons authorised to receive the information you normally send to your manager or supervisor? If not, who is authorised?
>
> _____

Typical faults with communication equipment

It could be that you have been given:

- a pager

- a mobile telephone

- a two-way radio.

Or you may simply have access to a land telephone. All of this type of equipment can fail unexpectedly. This will create problems with your ability to communicate. It will also mean that you are unable to pass on information and others will be unable to pass information on to you. There may also be health and safety or security concerns if the communication equipment has failed.

Reporting the faults

Some companies will have set procedures for reporting faults with communication equipment. They may have a contract with service engineers, or contractors. These people come out and deal with the situation for the company. Sometimes you will have to contact an authorised person, who will organise the repair of the communication equipment. Sometimes the responsibility will be for the company you work for. At other times it will be the workplace that takes on this responsibility.

TASK

What is the procedure in your workplace for reporting problems with communication equipment?

_____

_____

_____

Being aware of your customers

There is a saying that 'the customer is always right'. This means that you are there for the customer. You must try to do whatever they request, within reason. Occasionally customers can be unreasonable and demanding. You may have a work routine and need to complete particular tasks by a certain time. This sometimes makes it difficult to respond to what customers want when they want it.

Customer needs and attitudes

From time to time, customers may ask you to break from your normal work routine. They may want you to carry out tasks that are not normally a part of your job. Each time this happens, you will need to make a judgement as to whether:

- it is a reasonable request
- there is time to do it
- you need to check with your supervisor before you do anything.

At times customers might be:

- angry and unreasonable – you should be polite and patient
- demanding – stay calm and do as much as you can
- bossy – politely explain you have a job to do as well.

TASK

☐ Have you had to deal with difficult customers and how did you respond?

_____

_____

_____

☐ Why do you think this was the right way to respond?

_____

_____

_____

Chapter 2

Communication

57

Your own response

In most situations you should be able to establish customer needs and attitudes and respond yourself. Most customers are not unreasonable or too demanding. They are usually delighted if you can respond positively to their needs and attitudes. It should not upset your working day too much if you are a little flexible at times. You need to make sure that:

● you are clear about what the customer wants

● it is reasonable for you to do it

● you have time to do it.

It is all about give and take. But remember to stay calm, smile, be polite and give a good impression, in whatever way you have to respond.

Getting help in responding

Sometimes it is not possible for you to make a decision without asking for help. Perhaps what the customer is asking is too unreasonable or will take too long. It may not even be a part of your job. You must know whom to contact to get advice. Others doing the same job as you may have had similar problems in the past. The person you contact may have a company procedure to follow in situations such as this.

Knowledge test

1 **When a person receiving a communication lets the sender know they have understood, what is their reply or response known as?**

   a. Non-verbal.

   b. Information.

   c. Explanation.

   d. Feedback.

2 **Good communication in teams is important because:**

   a. they can share ideas.

   b. they become more efficient.

   c. they can share information.

   d. All of the above.

3 **Which one of the following should you NOT do when speaking to someone face-to-face?**

   a. Pay attention.

   b. Stare.

   c. Smile.

   d. Nod your head.

4 **When speaking to someone on the telephone which of these should you NOT do?**

   a. Confirm you understand.

   b. Repeat what they have said to show you understand.

   c. Follow-up on their request.

   d. Ignore what they have said.

5 **You represent your company so you should never be:**

   a. polite.

   b. clear.

   c. helpful.

   d. rude.

6 **Which of the following does NOT create a positive image?**

   a. Clean and tidy personal protective equipment.

   b. Poor personal hygiene.

   c. Politeness.

   d. Good communication.

7 **Which one of the following is NOT a verbal source of information for your job?**

   a. Your supervisor.

   b. Your team members.

   c. Your client.

   d. Your staff handbook.

8 **Which one of the following is NOT a written form of communication?**

   a. Email.

   b. Report.

   c. Handbook.

   d. Telephone conversation.

9 **What is the term used to describe a file of instructions or ways of doing things?**

   a. Staff newsletter.

   b. Memorandum.

   c. Staff handbook.

   d. Business letter.

10 **What are procedures?**

   a. Set ways of doing things.

   b. Information about meetings.

   c. Files containing information.

   d. Notes about customers.

11 What kind of document would be sent to particular members of staff with information to help them do their job?

a. A newsletter.

b. A report.

c. A form.

d. A memorandum.

12 Which one of the following is an example of verbal communication?

a. A telephone conversation.

b. A discussion.

c. A meeting.

d. All of the above.

13 Which of the following is a formal written communication?

a. Email.

b. Report.

c. Note.

d. Message.

14 Smiles and hand gestures are examples of what type of communication?

a. Written.

b. Verbal.

c. Non-verbal.

d. None of the above.

15 If a client is angry you should not:

a. be polite.

b. stay calm.

c. be patient.

d. ignore them.

16 What is another word used to describe something that you might use up and have to replace from time to time?

a. Edible.

b. Material.

c. Consumable.

d. Recordable.

17 What word is used to describe someone who is entitled to see particular information?

a. Authorised.

b. Supervised.

c. Prioritised.

d. Recognised.

18 Which one of the following is NOT a problem in passing on information?

a. You don't know who to tell.

b. You don't have the information.

c. You only have part of the information.

d. You know exactly what to say and to whom.

19 Which one of the following is not a written form of communication?

a. Body language.

b. Email.

c. Cleaning agent instructions on a bottle.

d. Work schedule.

20 Non-verbal communication includes:

a. facial expressions.

b. gestures.

c. eye contact.

d. All of the above.

Chapter 3

Working in teams and developing yourself

What you will learn:

- How to work effectively with others
- Welcoming new team members
- Sharing knowledge and skills
- Answering questions and providing help
- Handling disagreements
- Reporting disagreements
- Customer requirements and responding
- Developing yourself in your job
- Setting realistic targets
- Work activities and support
- Reviewing and updating progress
- Discussing progress with supervisors and colleagues

What makes an effective team?

A good team is one whose members:

- co-operate with each other
- agree on what should be done
- communicate well with each other (see Communication, Chapter 2)
- work well together
- make the best use of their time
- make the best use of their **resources**
- support one another
- make the best use of individual skills.

> **DEFINITION**
>
> **Resources**
>
> Resources are people, equipment and materials that are used to do a job.

Being part of a team is rewarding.

Being part of a team

Being a member of a team can be very rewarding. You can share ideas, identify the resources that you need and agree how the work will be split. You should try to contribute to the team you belong to as much as possible. You should offer ideas or solutions to problems. You should also try to support your colleagues as much as you can.

Most of us have skills that we are proud of. Working in a team gives you a chance to use your skills to benefit the whole team.

However, one member of a team may not have all the skills required to carry out a task. This is where colleagues with the other required skills can help.

Welcoming new team members

A positive attitude and being friendly is welcoming to new team members.

TASK

☐ What tasks in your job can be shared with other members of your team?

_____

_____

_____

Welcoming others

From time to time new people will join your team. They need to be able to fit in quickly and feel welcome. You can help them feel welcome by having a positive attitude (see Communication, pages 34–37) towards them and being friendly and supportive. You will also need to be efficient and business-like. Remember that they are new, so sometimes you need to be understanding. Be open with them and honest. Members of a team need to trust one another and co-operate. This will make the team work as effectively as possible.

Telling them what they need to know

Every job has its own procedures and basic work routines. Newcomers to the team need to pick these up quickly. They will then be able to contribute to the team effort. If people do not know what is expected of them, you cannot always expect them to do the right thing, at the right time and in the right way. People need to know:

- where equipment and materials are kept

- the order in which they should do work

- the quality of work the customer expects

- whom to ask for help if they have problems

- what everybody else in the team does.

TASK

☐ Try to remember what it was like when you first joined your team. What things did you need to know?

_____

_____

_____

☐ How helpful were your team members?

_____

_____

_____

Demonstrating jobs to others

Demonstrating a job may mean showing someone how to use equipment or how to use cleaning products safely. Usually, there will be some time for a newcomer to the team to be shown how to do things. The team member who is the most expert is often chosen to demonstrate, or the supervisor may do it. If you are asked to show them how to do a task, remember:

> **DEFINITION**
>
> **Demonstrating**
>
> Demonstrating means showing someone how a task is done.

- health and safety is important
- don't agree to demonstrate anything unless you are confident about it yourself
- if you can't demonstrate, tell them who can (see 'Knowing your limits', page 66)
- if you can, be patient and show them slowly
- repeat each step to make sure they understand
- let them try and tell them if they make a mistake.

Assisting your colleagues

Some jobs are one-person tasks. Other jobs can be completed more efficiently if you all work together. It is also true that if you are able to help a colleague by showing them a better way to do their job, you should share your skills and experience with them. Most people welcome advice and help. In return, there may be things they can do to help you.

TASK

☐ In which areas of your work are you able to assist your colleagues?

_____

_____

_____

Dealing with questions and helping out

Sharing the work and co-operation are vital parts of an **efficient** team. But it is also about sharing your skills and knowledge. Less experienced team members will often ask questions, or request help. You could be the ideal person to assist them. You may have had similar questions yourself in the past. You may have needed help from others. Always be prepared to share your experiences and try to help when you can. This makes for a much more efficient team and a friendlier place to work.

Knowing your limits

Sometimes you may just be too busy to help. You may not even think that it is your job to help out. Your colleague may be asking you something that you are not really sure about, or it is not your responsibility.

Know your limits:

- If you are unsure don't interfere.
- Direct the person to someone who can help.
- Apologise for not being able to help them.
- Explain why you can't help them.
- Check that they have been helped by someone else.

> **DEFINITION**
>
> **Efficient**
>
> Efficient means being able to complete a task to a specific standard in a timely manner.

Figure 3.1. It is important you know to whom you can direct colleaagues to ask for help.

TASK

☐ Someone has asked for your help and you are unsure of the answer or procedure to follow. Who would you direct the person to?

_____

Protecting the team

In all teams, there will always be some disagreements. The main thing is that these disagreements are sorted out as quickly as possible. It is not a good idea for a team to be working in a bad atmosphere. It is important that the team members can:

- be honest with one another
- be able to express their opinions without causing an argument
- be able to agree a solution
- stick to a solution once agreed
- not hold grudges.

Protecting your company

If team members argue with each other in front of customers or the public, it gives a very negative image of their company. Any disagreements should be handled in private and not in public places. Disagreements should certainly be sorted out away from customers. The team members should:

- agree to talk about the disagreement
- choose a time and place to talk
- always consider the image or reputation of the company
- always try to behave professionally (in a business-like way) in front of customers.

Common reasons for disagreements in teams are:

- criticising another team member to an outsider
- leaving a team member out by not telling them something or deciding something without asking them
- not sorting out the situation if someone dislikes another team member
- saying something hurtful
- deliberately being awkward or unpleasant
- over-reacting to something
- not sorting out a small problem before it becomes a major problem.

Figure 3.2. *It is important that disagreements are discussed and resolved away from the public eye.*

TASK

If you are having a disagreement at work, whom should you talk to about the issue? Circle the correct answer and explain why.

☐ A customer   ☐ Your supervisor   ☐ A security person

_____

_____

_____

When to report a disagreement

Sometimes there will be disagreements that the team members cannot resolve between themselves. Perhaps the disagreement is too serious, or the team just can't come up with a solution. This could cause problems, affect the work of the team and make people unhappy. When it gets to this stage, someone else has to be involved. You need to report the disagreement, so that someone else can try to come up with a solution.

Disagreements should be reported when:

- the team members still disagree after trying to resolve the issue
- the team members have tried everything they could to make things work
- the team is not working well as a unit
- someone in the team is very unhappy.

Knowing whom to report to

All companies and workplaces have procedures (see Health and safety responsibilities, page 3) for dealing with disagreements. Usually you would report a disagreement to one of the following:

- your team leader
- your supervisor
- your manager.

You should not involve your customers or anyone from outside the company or workplace in a disagreement involving your team. A team disagreement is for the team and the company to sort out.

TASK

☐ What procedure does your company or workplace expect you to follow if you have a disagreement?

_____

_____

_____

Asking for help

There may be times when you need help from other people. Sometimes you will need to ask another member of the team. Or perhaps you have to ask your team leader, supervisor or manager. At other times you might have to ask the customer for help. It is important that you should always be polite and grateful for their assistance. You should not demand anyone's help, but request it. People will be far more willing to help if you have shown them that you appreciate their assistance.

Choosing the right moment

If you are busy or rushing to get something done you would not appreciate someone demanding your attention or asking for help. So you must choose the right moment to ask for help. Always:

- ask if it is a convenient time
- don't interrupt if it is obvious they are busy
- apologise for disturbing them
- ask them the question as simply as possible
- listen carefully to their response
- thank them for their help.

TASK

- Think about the times you have had to ask for help. Who have you turned to?

  _____

- How helpful have they been?

  _____

- Would they have been more or less helpful if you had asked in a different way or at a different time?

  _____

Listening to customers

Your customers will often have preferred ways in which they want certain tasks to be done. Some things will be more important to them than others. This might mean that you will have to change the order in which you do work, or it might mean changing your priorities. This means doing things that are less important to you first, because they may be more important for the customer.

DEFINITION

Cleaning standards

Cleaning standards are the minimum acceptable level of work that a company wishes to provide for its customers.

Remember, the customer is paying for the service you are providing. They have the right to ask for things to be done in a certain way, as long as they bear in mind your company's **cleaning standards** and procedures, and all health and safety requirements and regulations. You should:

- listen to your customers' requests carefully
- ask questions to make sure you have understood what they want
- tell them you will do your best to match their requirements if possible.

Figure 3.3. You should respect customers' requests. But always check with your supervisor if you think it might mean breaking your company's rules.

Chapter 3

Working in teams and developing yourself

Responding to customers' requirements

It might be that your customer's requirements are reasonable and it would not affect what you do very much. If this is so, you can confirm directly to the customer that you will do it.

At other times, a customer's requirements might mean a major change in your work. So you will need to speak to your supervisor or someone else from your company or workplace. Check with them that it is acceptable for you to match the customer's requirements.

In all cases you must:

- tell the customer what you intend to do

- make sure anyone else involved is aware of the changes

- if you have passed on the customer's request to your company, tell the customer what information you have received.

Ensuring that customers' requirements have been met

It will be rare to be thanked by a customer, even if you have sorted out a problem. To make sure they are satisfied you should:

- agree with the customer what you have offered to do

- make sure what you have offered to do is acceptable to them – try to improve on this by doing something more

- make sure that if you have promised something by a particular time or date that it is done

- make sure that the quality of what you have offered to do is acceptable – would you find it acceptable if you were the customer?

Joining in discussions

Whenever a discussion takes place about the work you or your team is doing, some new decisions might be made. These could affect you.

The discussion might be about:

- splitting up the work
- taking on more responsibilities
- changes in the priorities that you should work to
- the equipment and materials you use
- comments and ideas from customers.

Other things that might be discussed are:

- changes in procedures (see Health and safety for the cleaning and support services industry, page 3)
- the best way to pass on information and act on it.

All of these things matter and if you have an opinion or an idea you should contribute to the discussion.

Why your ideas matter

You are one of the people who actually do the job. You are part of the team. So your knowledge about the work is valuable. You may have some good ideas about improving the quality of the work, the efficiency of the team, better procedures or ways of doing things.

Contributing to a discussion shows that you have thought about it and that you care.

TASK

☐ Are there opportunities for you to discuss your work? Who organises these discussions?

_____

_____

_____

☐ Are your ideas welcomed? Has anything changed as a result of one of your suggestions?

_____

_____

_____

Identifying and explaining areas for self-development

Self-development is about making sure your skills are up to date. Think about your current skills and interests. This should not only give you a good idea about what you are good at, but also what skills you would like to learn.

The idea is to create a plan that identifies your learning needs and your goals for the future. Try writing down what you are learning from your daily work experiences. In which areas would you like to develop more skills? These could be areas that you are particularly interested in, or ones that you do not feel so comfortable doing.

Figure 3.4. Consider your goals for the future.

📖 DEFINITION

Self-development

Self-development is about taking personal responsibility for your own learning and development.

Agreeing areas for self-development

Self-development can be useful for your future career. But you will need to find someone who can give you support, advice and assistance. The person should look through your self-development ideas and give you advice on how best to achieve them.

TASK

Write down all the skills you use daily on a separate sheet of paper.

Then answer the following questions:

☐ What are my strengths (things you are good at doing)?

_____

_____

☐ What are my weaknesses (what things do you not do so well)?

_____

_____

☐ What do I hope to improve and achieve?

_____

_____

☐ Why do I want to achieve that? How can I do it?

_____

_____

How to set targets

You need to make sure that any **targets** you set yourself are achievable.

- Think about your present situation. How much can you do now?

- Set targets a little higher than your present skills and experience. Then aim for these.

> **DEFINITION**
>
> **Targets**
>
> Targets are set goals and ambitions that you aim to achieve within a given time period.

Remember that your targets have a cost. It might be time, energy or even relationships. If the cost might be too great you may have to rethink your target.

You need to set a balance between setting an achievable target and stretching yourself.

Why is it important that your targets are realistic?

If your targets are too ambitious or too high, you might struggle to achieve them or you might not achieve them at all. When people do not achieve their targets they often feel they have failed themselves. That is why it is far better to set targets as one small step at a time. In other words, you need to set yourself goals that will push you rather than disappoint you.

TASK

☐ Think about one of the targets you listed in the previous activity. What is a realistic deadline to set for achieving this target?

_____

☐ How long do you think it will realistically take you?

_____

☐ What might you have to give up to reach this target?

_____

_____

Work activities for self-development

Your self-development plan needs to involve doing things and then reviewing what you have done. Each of the activities needs to have a purpose and a goal. You need to work towards your goals one at a time to reach your long-term aims. You have to take responsibility to identify activities that will stretch you. Select activities that give you the opportunity to stretch those new skills you are developing.

Support needed to achieve targets

Many companies and workplaces are very supportive of their staff when it comes to learning and development. By working out your own self-development plan, you will have shown them that you are serious. They will be more likely now to offer their help. Your team members, supervisor, manager, workplace, local learning centre are all valuable sources of support and advice. Also, learning is far more flexible these days. So try to find a programme that suits your own needs.

Reviewing and updating progress

One useful way of keeping track of your self-development is to set dates for achieving your targets. You can review your targets as the dates come up. You can also change the dates if necessary or set more dates for the next stage of your development.

By regularly **reviewing** your progress you will be able to see where you are ahead and where you are falling behind. You can then make a decision about your priorities. Or you could come up with another way of achieving those targets on time.

There is no use in setting a self-development plan and then ignoring it, hoping that you will achieve the target by magic.

Procedures for reviewing and updating

If you have agreed a self-development plan with your company or workplace then they will set aside time for regular review and updating meetings. This will usually be carried out by your supervisor or manager. Together you can discuss your progress. They may suggest how you could have achieved the targets that you found difficult. They can also advise you about your next set of targets and when these should be achieved.

> ### DEFINITION
>
> **Reviewing**
>
> Reviewing is looking back on your work performance and targets to:
>
> - check if you had achieved what you had aimed for
> - assess how you can complete your targets
> - check what you could have done better.

Figure 3.5. Reviewing progress with your employer is a valuable activity.

TASK

How can your company or workplace help you set and develop your own personal targets and learning goals?

_____

_____

_____

Requesting feedback

Each time you take part in activities, and use skills that you have developed, try to get the opinion of others about your performance. This is known as feedback (see Communication, page 32). You can use their comments to help you improve your performance in the future. Every bit of advice when you are using new skills is valuable. Not only will it give you extra confidence but it can also help you identify things that you have not got quite right as yet and upon which you can improve.

The benefits of discussing progress

Formal feedback about your performance is useful. But you can also benefit from discussing your progress with other members of your team. They will be able to notice improvements that you have made and be able to put you right on things you may be doing wrong. Your supervisor will also be able to help. They should also provide you with encouragement to keep taking part in activities that use these new skills.

TASK

☐ Give three benefits of requesting feedback and discussing progress.

1 _____

2 _____

3 _____

1 **What word is used to describe people, equipment and materials that are used to do a job?**

   a. Items.

   b. Resources.

   c. Materials.

   d. Skills.

2 **Which one of the following is a valuable reason for being part of a team?**

   a. Sharing ideas.

   b. Making cups of tea.

   c. Identifying the resources you need.

   d. Going for drinks after work.

3 **When welcoming a new member of the team should you:**

   a. be friendly and helpful?

   b. be quiet?

   c. be rude and unfriendly?

   d. ignore them?

4 **If a new team member asks a question that you are unable to answer, as the first thing, should you:**

   a. guess the answer?

   b. make something up?

   c. tell them you don't know?

   d. direct them to your supervisor?

5 **You have to ask your customer for help. Which one of the following should you NOT do?**

   a. Ask if it is convenient for them to talk to you.

   b. Interrupt them while they are talking with someone else.

   c. Apologise for disturbing them.

   d. Thank them for their help.

6 **Which one of these would be an inappropriate request from a customer?**

   a. Stand on a chair to clean some loose shelving.

   b. Replace the soap in the ladies' washroom.

   c. Carefully remove some broken glass in a labelled bag.

   d. Vacuum clean a carpeted area.

7 **Which one of the following is NOT valuable to a discussion?**

   a. Your knowledge of your job.

   b. Your ideas about improving the work schedule.

   c. Your ideas for better work procedures.

   d. Your thoughts on how a colleague dresses.

8 **Which one of these is part of a self-development plan?**

   a. Reasons why you left your last job.

   b. Your learning needs.

   c. Your salary.

   d. Your holiday entitlement.

9 **The best person to help with your self-development plan is someone who:**

   a. can get you to work on time.

   b. is fun to work with.

   c. is honest and rude.

   d. can offer support, advice and guidance.

10 Which one of the following is a valuable source of advice to discuss your self-development plan and targets?

a. Your best friend.

b. The lady who works in reception.

c. Your supervisor.

d. Your mum.

11 What word is used to describe showing someone else how to do something?

a. Confiscate.

b. Demonstrate.

c. Activate.

d. Participate.

12 Which one of the following is a vital part of an efficient team?

a. Sharing the work.

b. Co-operating with other team members.

c. Sharing skills.

d. All of the above.

13 When someone asks for help and you are not sure about it, which one of the following should you NOT do?

a. Direct them to someone who can help.

b. Apologise for not being able to help.

c. Ignore them.

d. Explain why you can't help.

14 Your team has a major disagreement. Which one of the following people should you NOT involve?

a. Your team leader.

b. Your customer.

c. Your supervisor.

d. Your manager.

15 Self-development is about taking personal responsibility for:

a. your job.

b. your role.

c. your learning.

d. your equipment.

16 Which one of the following words best describes the targets you should set for your self-development?

a. Optimistic.

b. Realistic.

c. Pessimistic.

d. Sympathetic.

17 Self-development involves doing things and then:

a. repeating what you have done.

b. reporting what you have done.

c. reviewing what you have done.

d. forgetting what you have done.

Chapter 3

Working in teams and developing yourself

18 **What should you set to help you check your self-development progress?**

a. Targets.

b. Penalties.

c. Excuses.

d. Strategies.

19 **When people give you advice and their opinion after they have watched your performance, what is this called?**

a. Interference.

b. Nosiness.

c. Feedback.

d. Obstruction.

20 **Self-development is:**

a. your own learning and development.

b. the learning of your team.

c. getting a job.

d. adhering to a work schedule.

Chapter 4

Dealing with routine and non-routine waste

What you will learn:

- What is meant by waste?
- Types of waste
- Waste and recycling
- The procedures for preparing your work area
- Approved methods for transferring waste

- Recording waste
- How to deal with waste containers
- How to handle non-routine waste
- Disposal of special non-routine waste

What is meant by waste?

It is a requirement under the Health and Safety at Work etc. Act 1974 that every business or company must handle, store and dispose of **waste** properly.

This includes the following:

- Products whose date for appropriate use has expired, e.g. food that has passed its 'use by' date.

- Material spilled and lost, and any materials, equipment, etc. contaminated as a result of the accident.

- Materials contaminated or soiled as a result of planned actions, e.g. leftover material (residues) from cleaning operations, packaging materials, containers, etc.

- Unusable parts e.g. reject or used batteries.

- Substances that no longer perform satisfactorily, e.g. floor polish that has become rancid (bad).

- Residues from processes that aim to reduce pollution, e.g. spent filters.

> **DEFINITION**
>
> **Waste**
>
> Waste is defined in the Environment Act 1995 as: 'Any substance or object which the holder discards or intends to, or is required to discard.'

The main legislation (rules and regulations) covering waste management is the Environmental Protection Act 1990. Everyone has a 'duty of care' to ensure you manage your waste so that it does not harm human health or the environment. To do so, you must:

- store waste safely and securely

- recover and recycle packaging

- dispose of hazardous waste (see page 101) by having it removed and treated or disposed of, by licensed contractors at licensed waste sites and facilities. (If hazardous waste is not disposed of correctly it can be a source of disease-causing germs and physical contamination.)

Other legislation includes:

- HSE Approved Code of Practice

- Water Supply Regulations 1999

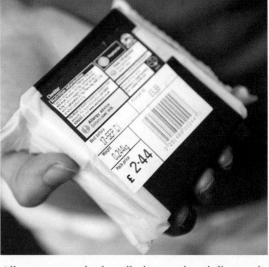

All waste must be handled, stored and disposed of correctly.

What is meant by waste?

All companies need to carry out risk assessments (see Health safety and security, pages 4–6) for the disposal and storage of waste to identify how high the risk is in each area of the premises.

RISK ASSESSMENT FORM

SITE:	All	DEPARTMENT:	ALL		HoD:	
ACTIVITY:	Manual handling including lifting lowering, pushing, pulling, moving, carrying etc.	ASSESSMENT COMPLETED BY:				

HAZARD REF NO	HAZARD	WHO IS AT RISK	HOW MANY	HOW OFTEN	EXISTING CONTROLS	POTENTIAL HARM	CHANCE OF HARM	OVERALL RISK
1	Back Strain	-	-	-	Avoid manual handling where possible, if beyond own lifting capacity use lifting aids where practicable and possible (e.g. forklift trucks, hoists etc.). Operatives reminded of correct lifting techniques.	Serious	Possible	Medium
2	Foot Injury	-	-	-	Toe protection footwear to be worn.	Minor	Possible	Low
3	Hand Injury	-	-	-	Gloves provided and worn.	Minor	Possible	Low

HAZARD REF NO	ACTION REQUIRED	RESPONSIBLIITY	TARGET DATE	COMPLETION DATE
1	Ensure manual handling training provided. Provide lifting aids of the type that are fit for the purpose of the task.	Line Manager	Soon as possible	
2&3	Ensure Toe protection footwear and gloves are provided and worn	Line Manager	Soon as possible	

Figure 4.1. Risk assessment forms should be completed if the company has 5 or more employees, be up to date and reviewed and identify protective and preventative measures.

The Controlled Waste Regulations 1992 offers guidance on how to dispose of waste properly to avoid:

- pest infestation (see page 97)

- accidents

- an unpleasant build-up of waste and to minimise health hazards (see Health safety and security, page 4).

Other reasons for disposing of waste in an organised way are:

- to avoid security problems

- to prevent cross-contamination

- to make it easy to collect (too much waste in one area may cause problems with lifting and handling).

DEFINITION

Pests

Pests include rats, mice and many insects, such as cockroaches and flies.

Dealing with routine and non-routine waste

Types of waste

Waste can be divided into two main types: routine and non-routine waste.

Routine waste

The majority of routine waste is domestic (household) waste, such as cooked food waste, paper, cans, bottles, etc.

Other routine waste is commercial waste, such as large quantities of cardboard, cartridges, etc.

Non-routine waste

Non-routine waste can be classified as:

- hazardous
- clinical
- confidential
- unidentifiable
- mixed.

It is very important that you learn how to identify and categorise waste. This will help you deal with different kinds of waste appropriately. This involves knowing how to:

- handle the waste safely
- collect and transfer it in the correct way
- separate it according to regulations and instructions.

Some waste has to be disposed of in a particular way, such as hazardous waste or clinical waste (see pages 101–102). If there is any waste you cannot identify or you believe may be hazardous, you must ask your supervisor for advice.

There is also a risk to the environment from the incorrect storage and disposal of waste. For example, paper could be a fire hazard if it is allowed to collect.

Paper will burn easily.

TASK

☐ What are the procedures followed by your company, and what is the required equipment for handling and disposing of the type of waste you are dealing with?

_____

_____

_____

Waste and recycling

With increased general interest in climate change and the environment, more companies are ensuring that their employees follow environmentally friendly practices. Most companies now aim to improve their waste management practices from time to time. This is by:

- firstly, reducing the amount of waste produced
- secondly, re-using and **recycling** as much as possible
- and as a last resort, disposal to landfill.

There are several more reasons for doing this:

- To comply with health and safety regulations including the Environment Protection Act 1990
- As a cost-cutting exercise
- As a way of reducing waste removal costs, especially where there is a possibility to be charged by weight of refuse in the future
- As a way of making money out of waste and donating to charities. (This could be seen as a marketing or public relations exercise where the company is supporting a well-known charity.)

Recycling waste means that fewer new products need to be made, which saves raw materials and energy consumption. Some of the materials we can recycle are paper, plastics, metals (such as aluminium tins) and tyres.

Waste paper can be put back into the pulping system and recycled as more paper. Nowadays, 50 per cent of the paper waste produced by the newspaper industry is being recycled. Special bins and containers are often provided for waste paper in offices.

The largest producers of waste glass and bottles are hotels and pubs. The majority of used glass and bottles is collected in bottle banks. Bottle banks can be clear, brown and green in colour. Only the correct coloured bottles should be put in each coloured bank. The UK currently recycles one-third of its glass. This is far behind other European countries where 80 per cent of glass is recycled.

DEFINITION

Recycling

Recycling is processing used materials into new products to prevent waste of potentially useful materials. However, even if material is sent for recycling or undergoes treatment in-house, it can still be waste.

DEFINITION

Waste recycling

The collection, separation and clean up of those materials that can be re-used is called waste recycling.

Dealing with routine and non-routine waste

Waste and recycling

Plastics make up a large percentage of waste in the form of packaging. Packaging can be recycled easily by melting and moulding. Plastic waste tends to be sorted by hand. In the UK, three per cent of plastic is recycled. In Germany, 70 per cent is recycled.

> ☐☐ **DEFINITION**
>
> **Cost-effective**
>
> Cost-effective is, in this context, when the value of the waste when it has been recycled is higher than the cost of recycling.

Aluminium recycling is very popular in the UK. Aluminium is an expensive metal and therefore can be very **cost-effective** when recycled. At present in the UK, a third of aluminium cans are recycled. In Australia and America, over two-thirds are recycled.

Twenty-one per cent of old tyres are re-treaded and re-used but almost half are sent to landfill sites. (Source: www.defra.gov.uk/environment/waste/topics/index.htm and The Manchester College)

Many companies now have different coloured waste bins, which are clearly labelled as to which type of waste should be disposed in them. There are usually separate bins for cans, paper and card, and general waste. Detergents and chemicals are never recycled as they are considered to be hazardous waste (see page 101).

Waste bins are different colours and clearly labelled which type of waste should be disposed of in them.

Waste and recycling

TASK

What are the arrangements for recycling in your workplace?

_____

_____

_____

TASK

Complete the table giving four examples of the type waste to be recycled and what new products can be made from it.

Type of waste	New product

Dealing with routine and non-routine waste

The procedures for preparing your work area

Before handling waste of any kind you must make sure you are wearing the correct personal protective equipment (PPE; see Health and safety for the cleaning and support services industry page 8 and also see the following section).

You should collect everything you need and take it to the area where you are working to save time and to work in a tidy manner.

Your equipment may include:

- different coloured waste bags

- bin liners

- a warning sign

- a clean cloth and detergent to wash any dirty containers or a pressure washer, depending on location and size of waste container

- a trolley to transfer the waste from the collection area to outside containers.

If any waste is spilled on the floor, you may also need a mop and bucket to clean it up immediately. However, if you are not sure what the spillage is then you must check with your supervisor about the best way to clean up the spillage.

Remember that if you are working in different areas then you must use colour-coded equipment to prevent cross-contamination (see Health safety and security, page 6).

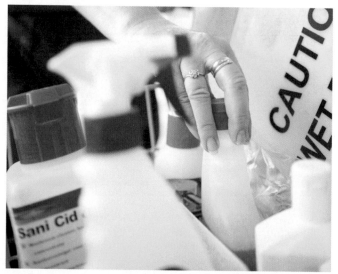

It is important you collect the correct materials and equipment before starting your work.

Wearing the correct personal protective equipment

When you are preparing to collect, sort or separate routine waste from an area, make sure you are wearing the correct PPE. This should have been provided for you by your company. You need to wear the correct PPE to protect yourself and others from possible injury and infection.

PPE you need to wear will include your uniform and also gloves and strong shoes. You may also carry litter picking tongs, depending on your role.

The procedures for preparing your work area

You may also need to check your workplace instructions for handling routine waste and seek advice from your supervisor on any additional PPE that may be required.

Note: The Health and Safety at Work Act etc. 1974 states that anyone who has caused an injury or harm to health to themselves or someone else because they were not wearing the correct PPE provided by their employer could be heavily fined or even be sent to prison.

It is vital you wear the correct PPE.

TASK

List three items of Personal Protective Equipment (PPE). Explain when and why each item should be used.

Item of PPE	When to use it	Why it should be used

TASK

What is the correct PPE for your working environment and why?

_____

_____

_____

The importance of personal hygiene

Good personal hygiene (see Health safety and security, page 10) helps to prevent cross-contamination (see Health safety and security, page 6) and the spread of germs that cause infection from one area to another. It also helps you to protect yourself from catching infections.

You should always wash and dry your hands using clean running water, soap and paper towels before:

- eating
- drinking
- smoking
- using a phone
- taking medication
- inserting contact lenses
- wearing protective gloves
- handling waste of any kind.

You should also wash your hands again after doing any of the above, and particularly after removing your gloves or using the toilet.

Washing your hands is an important part of maintaining personal hygiene.

TASK

Fill in the blank in the following sentence:

☐ Personal hygiene helps prevent _____ spreading from one place to another.

Approved methods for transferring waste

You need to separate and sort each type of waste in a safe way by placing it in separate containers to avoid injury to yourself or others. To do this, you should follow these guidelines:

- Wet waste, which is usually food waste, should be separated from dry waste.

- Dry waste may have a salvage value (this means that it could be sold to a recycling company, which may then treat it (melt it down) and then sell it to another company for re-use). The actual amount of money received for it may not be its true value. An example of this is copper cooking utensils which have been melted down to provide for roofing materials. If it does not have any value it can be burnt on-site or removed by the local authority, although in some areas the council may make a charge to the company for removing it.

- Cans and bottles may be compacted (squashed) to aid temporary storage.

- Glass may be broken and must be kept separate from other types of waste.

- Aerosols are pressurised containers and should never be burnt as they will explode.

- The transferring of waste materials should be kept to a minimum to prevent the tearing of bags.

- You should not manually compact (squash) bags.

TASK

Why should all waste bags be clearly marked and labelled?

_____

_____

_____

- Ask your supervisor to whom you should report any spillages or inadequate packaging and how to contact them.

- Should there be a non-routine waste spillage then you should secure the area by cordoning it off or displaying warning signs.

- All bags to be transported should be put in wheeled or rigid containers. This will help to reduce a risk of hurting yourself through lifting heavy bags or injury from sharps.

Approved methods for transferring waste

- Bags must not be more than three-quarters full and tied at the neck and if possible double bagged. Waste bags should not be secured by wire or staples as this could cause injury to refuse collectors.

- Always remember that under the Health and Safety at Work etc. Act 1974 you have a duty of care to yourself and others to handle waste safely.

- You should handle bags by the neck and not drop or throw them.

Figure 4.2. Using wheeled containers helps prevent you injuring yourself.

TASK

☐ Describe how you would correctly lift a heavy bag.

_____

_____

_____

Figure 4.3. Suspicious packages or bags must always be reported.

Suspicious packages

It is your responsibility under the Heath and Safety at Work etc. Act 1974 to be aware of items left unsupervised or which look out of place (see Health safety and security, page 8).

Approved methods for transferring waste

TASK

▪ What is the procedure in your company or workplace for dealing with suspicious items?

_____

_____

_____

Waste collection points

It is also important to take waste to the right collection point for disposal. Failure to do this might mean that the waste is put in the wrong container or mixed with hazardous waste. You will then be putting yourself and others at risk from injury or infection. Always check your company's policy or ask your supervisor if you are unsure of where to dispose of certain waste.

Check that the contents of bags or containers are secure and make sure you are wearing the correct PPE (including gloves).

If the item is heavy or awkward to lift then you must use the correct lifting and handling technique. This is required according to the Manual Handling Operations Regulations 1992 (see Health and safety for the cleaning and support services industry page 12). If you are not sure, ask your supervisor to show you.

You should also make sure that the bags or containers have not been damaged during handling. When you have finished moving waste check that the bag or container is not damaged and report to your supervisor if it is.

All waste transferred off-site should be accompanied by a Waste Transfer Note. This note contains information in accordance with the relevant regulatory requirements of the Environmental Protection Act 1990. The information includes:

- description and quantity of waste

- a six-number European Waste Catalogue (EWC) code for the waste

- the type of container

- where the transfer took place

- the time and place of transfer

- the name and address of both persons involved in the transfer

- the registered waste carrier number.

Copies of Waste Transfer Notes should be available at all times. They should be retained for three years. This is because it may be necessary to prove where the waste came from and what was done with it.

Duty of care: Controlled waste transfer note

Description of waste

1. Description of the waste being transferred:

2. European Waste Catalogue Code:

3. How is the waste contained?
☐ Loose   ☐ Sacks   ☐ Skip   ☐ Drum   ☐ Other, please describe

4. What is the quantity of waste? (number of drums, tonnes etc.):

Current holder of the waste – *Transferor*

Full name:

Name and address of company:

Which of the following are you? *(one or more boxes may apply)*
☐ waste producer   ☐ holder of waste management licence   licence no:
                                                                             issued by:
☐ waste importer   ☐ exempt from waste management licence   reason why:
☐ waste collection authority   ☐ registered waste carrier   registration no:
                                                                             issued by:
☐ waste disposal authority   ☐ exempt from requirement to register   reason why:
  (Scotland only)

Person collecting the waste – *Transferee*

Full name:

Name and address of company:

Which of the following are you? *(one or more boxes may apply)*
☐ waste collection authority   ☐ authorised for transport purposes   specify purpose:
☐ waste disposal authority   ☐ holder of waste management licence   licence no:
  (Scotland only)   issued by:
                                    ☐ exempt from waste management licence   registration no:
                                    ☐ exempt from requirement to register   reason why:

Address of place of transfer

Date of transfer: Time of transfer (for multiple loads give between dates):

Name and address of broker (if applicable):

	TRANSFEROR	TRANSFEREE
Signature:		
Full name:		
Representing:		

Figure 4.4. Waste transfer notes records details about the waste.

TASK

Give three reasons why it is important to complete Waste Transfer Notes.

1 _____

2 _____

3 _____

How to deal with waste containers

It is important to clean the outside and inside of waste containers, and reline waste bins. This is done to:

- avoid bad smells by removing all signs of waste from the bin and surrounding areas

- reduce the risk of infection and disease by removing bits of remaining waste on which germs may grow

- avoid attracting **pests**, and create a pleasant and hygienic environment for yourself and the people you work with.

> **DEFINITION**
>
> **Pests**
>
> Pests include rats, mice and many insects, such as cockroaches and flies.

The hygienic disposal of waste is extremely important for the control of pests. The accumulation of food waste and greasy or sticky paper may attract rats and mice. It may also become the breeding ground for many insects, such as cockroaches and flies.

Without proper control, these pests can increase cross-contamination and spread disease. They can also cause costly damage to property. For example, rats and mice can gnaw through electric cables or products. Rats and mice make nests in stores of paper, boxes and old linen.

If you see any signs of pests having been around, you must tell your supervisor. For example you may have noticed droppings from rats or mice, holes in waste bags or you may have actually seen a pest.

- Germs can be passed from one pest to another and excreted by them onto food.

- Cross-contamination can occur from germs being left by pests on surfaces.

- Physical contamination can be from pests' bodies, for example their hair, droppings or eggs.

- Chemical contamination could come from careless use of insecticides (chemicals that kill insects) or from left over insecticide.

Food waste attracts pests.

TASK

☐ Why is it important to control pests?

_____

_____

_____

TASK

Complete the following table, listing four pests you are likely to see in your work area, where they are likely to be found and how you would control them.

Type of pest	Where likely to be found	How to control

TASK

☐ Why is it important to check waste bins for damage?

_____

_____

_____

The importance of keeping holding areas and waste containers clean

As explained above, it is important to have suitable locations for holding areas and collection bins under the Health and Safety at Work etc. Act 1974. This is to:

- avoid pest infestation (pests from being attracted to the waste)

- avoid accidents and injuries to yourself and other people

- avoid unpleasant build up of waste, and the associated problems of the appearance and smell of the waste

- minimise health hazards

- maintain security

- prevent cross-contamination

- make collection of waste easier.

TASK

Describe what you would do if you noticed that a waste container had blood on the outside.

_____

_____

_____

TASK

Why is it important to clean and/or reline waste collection bins?

_____

_____

_____

How to deal with waste containers

The following guidelines will help you make sure your waste storage areas are being used correctly:

- There should be no escape of waste from the container. If there are bits of waste sticking to the outside of the waste container, you should wash it thoroughly. If you are using a waste bag, double bag it.

- Any spillages should be reported and cleaned up immediately.

- Should there be a waste spillage, you should isolate the area by cordoning it off or displaying warning signs.

- Ask your supervisor to whom you should report any spillages or inadequate packaging and how to contact them.

- Check that waste has not blown away in bad weather.

- Check the condition of the waste containers for corrosion or damage. Report to your supervisor if found.

- Do not leave waste outside a skip.

- Check all skips are appropriately labelled.

- Lock all waste areas at night and over the weekends to prevent pests, animals or thieves entering.

- Do not mix hazardous and non-hazardous waste.

- Do not overfill a skip.

When you have emptied waste containers you should leave the containers clean and secure in the required place and in a condition that is fit for use.

You should then return all your equipment and materials to the appropriate storage area in a clean and safe condition. If necessary, wash your equipment to avoid cross-contamination and spread of infection.

You should also remove your PPE and dispose of your gloves correctly before leaving your workplace. The spread of infection often comes about from germs on the cleaning uniform being transferred to outside clothing.

Finally, wash your hands before leaving the premises.

TASK

Give two reasons why it is important to return all your equipment and cleaning materials in a clean and safe condition.

1 _____

2 _____

How to handle non-routine waste

Non-routine waste can be described as being:

- hazardous
- clinical
- confidential
- unidentifiable
- mixed.

Hazardous waste

Hazardous waste is waste that could cause harm. Hazardous waste includes all substances that are flammable, toxic corrosive or irritant. The storage, use and disposal of such substances is guided by the Control of Substances Hazardous to Health 1999 (COSHH) regulations (see Health safety and security, page 15).

It is a requirement of the Hazardous Waste Regulations 2005 that any company should register if it produces hazardous waste.

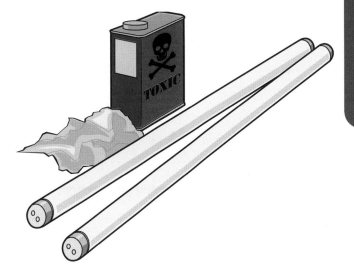

Figure 4.5. There are specific regulations related to the disposal of hazardous waste.

Reasons for materials being hazardous

- Spilled cooking oils make floors slippery and can block sinks.
- Sharps can cause cross-contamination and cuts.
- Incorrect disposal of waste water or cleaning agents can cause cross-contamination and they are a risk to the environment.
- Swabs/dressings can cause transfer of infection.
- Cans and bottles could cause cuts.
- Empty ink cartridges can cause a risk to the environment.
- Food waste is smelly and attracts pests.
- Rechargeable batteries can explode if heated and may contain mercury, which is hazardous.
- Lamps and fluorescent tubes also contain mercury.

TASK

☐ Give three examples of materials that may be hazardous.

1 _____

2 _____

3 _____

Clinical waste

Clinical waste includes waste from human or animal tissue, blood, excretion, body fluids, medicinal products, swabs, dressings, syringes, needles, sharps, or any other waste that may cause infections to a person coming into contact with it.

TASK

In the table below identify hazardous (H) and clinical (C) waste items.

Give reasons why you chose each type of waste.

	Type of waste (H/C)	Reason why it is H or C
Cooking oils		
Sharps (syringes, blades)		
Chemical waste		
Swabs and dressings		
Cans and bottles		
Empty ink cartridges		

Confidential waste

Confidential waste is any paper that contains confidential information, which will need to be burnt or shredded. It can give rise to identity theft (a type of crime in which someone pretends to be someone else in order to steal money or get other benefits). Sometimes files are left on the top of waste bins in an office by mistake. It could be that you may have thrown it away although it is something that is needed. So always check with your supervisor or ask the person whether they want to throw it away.

DEFINITION

Confidential

Confidential means that only certain people should be allowed to access or read the information.

I don't know what this is... what precautions should I take?

WARD 3

Figure 4.6. Always check if you are unsure if files are to be thrown away.

Unidentifiable substances

If you **do not know what a substance is**, you must assume that it is hazardous. Therefore you must inform your supervisor and obtain advice from them about how to deal with it.

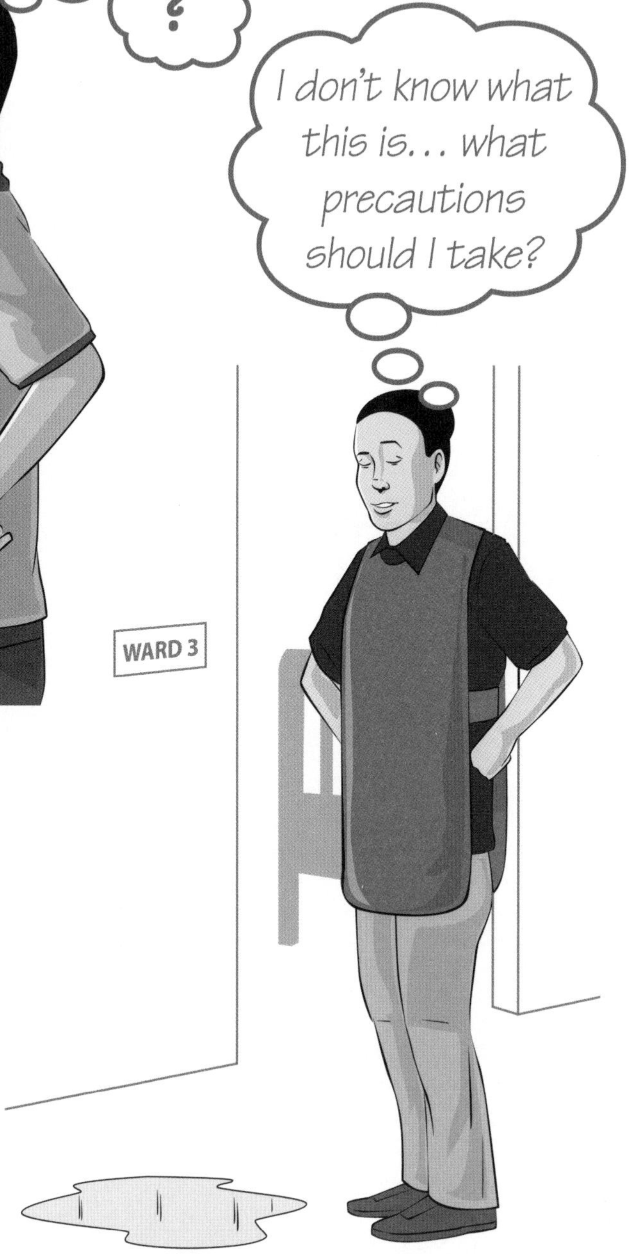

Figure 4.7. If you don't know what something is, assume that it is hazardous for your own and others' safety.

Mixed waste

Mixed waste may contain almost anything. And because it is mixed it may be hazardous. So again, you should report it to your supervisor for advice before handling it.

The mixing of non-hazardous and hazardous waste is banned under the Landfill Regulations 2002. If hazardous waste is found in a general waste skip, the whole contents become hazardous waste. In this case, your company will have to pay more for the higher costs of disposal.

The following list of items are now classified as hazardous waste:

- fridges and freezers
- motor vehicle tyres
- oils and oily rags
- tree roots
- asbestos
- chemicals
- computer monitors
- fluorescent tubes
- paint tins.

They must not be placed in any skip or other type of waste container.

Disposal of special non-routine waste

Clinical waste

As mentioned on page 102, clinical waste is waste contaminated with body fluids, such as swabs, dressings and disposable nappies. In high risk areas, such as isolation units in hospitals, all general waste must be regarded as infectious and treated as clinical waste.

Clinical waste must be placed in the correct colour-coded bag and securely sealed with the name of the clinical area for disposal. These bags will then be incinerated (burnt until it becomes ash). Black bags should only be used for non-hazardous household waste.

Used cloths or gloves which may be infected should be placed in a clinical bag and removed to be incinerated.

Chemical cleaning liquid waste should be disposed of down a foul water drain, i.e. a sluice or a toilet in extreme situations, not in an outside drain which is a rainwater drain. The drain should then be flushed out.

Clinical waste is a serious infection hazard for employees, customers, patients, the general public, the environment and waste-disposal contractors. It should only be removed from the premises and disposed of by licensed contractors. This is a requirement of the Waste Management Licensing Regulations 1994. The licensed contractor should arrange weekly collections of the plastic incinerator bins, replacing them with clean empty ones.

TASK

☐ What are the correct methods for handling and disposing of clinical waste?

_____

_____

_____

Sharps

Sharps must be disposed of with care as they can cause injury and carry the risk of infection. Be careful particularly when cleaning hand wash basins as they can be hidden in the overflow or in the plug hole. Use collection tweezers to pick up sharps. They do not need to be wrapped before placing in a sharps container.

DEFINITION

Sharps

Sharps are instruments such as needles, syringes or blades, which could pierce your skin or PPE. This means they could potentially cause injury or pass on infection.

Disposal of special non-routine waste

Sharps bins should conform to BS7320 and UN3291 standards. The British Standards (BS) and United Nations (UN) Standards describe the colour, markings and strength of containers which can be used for sharps.

Sharps bins are treated as clinical waste no matter where they are found. Prior to collection, the sharps bins must have their closures secured and the tops secured with adhesive packaging tape. They are disposed of via incineration. The remains of the incineration go to landfill. If there is no sharps container available, use the collection tweezers provided and place sharps in a glass jar or drinks can instead. The container should then be wrapped in a plastic bag and sealed with sticky tape and labelled 'Sharps'.

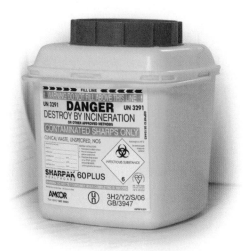

Sharps bins must conform to specific standards.

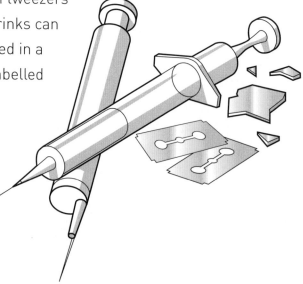

Figure 4.8. All 'sharps' must be placed in a sharps container to avoid injury to yourself or others.

TASK

- What is your workplace procedure on disposing of sharps?

  _____

  _____

- Why is it vital that you follow this procedure?

  _____

  _____

Sanitary towels and tampons

Where special disposal bins are provided, these should be used in preference to other methods of disposal. Where no special bin is provided and where flushing is not acceptable a sanitary towel or tampon should be placed in a small plastic bag and disposed of in the yellow clinical waste bag. This will then be incinerated.

Sani-bins or sanitation bins are small metal or plastic containers with lids. They are found in toilets for the collection of soiled sanitary towels. It is important that the bins are emptied frequently and kept clean.

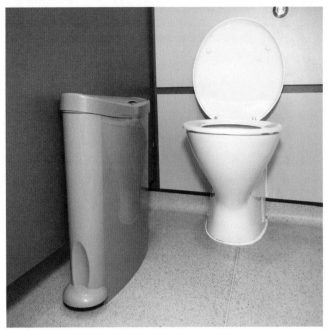

Sanitary bins must be emptied frequently.

Paper bags are often provided for the wrapping of soiled towels. In some places, there are incinerators that burn the towels leaving a small amount of ash which is removed during cleaning. Alternatively, there may be a container with germicidal fluid into which the soiled towels are placed. These containers are on loan and changed regularly.

Knowledge test

General issues regarding waste and dealing with routine waste

1 **Why should PPE be worn when at work?**

   a. To avoid damage to my clothes.

   b. So that I can be easily identified by strangers.

   c. To prevent an injury.

   d. So that my supervisor can see what I am doing.

2 **Which one of the following should be worn when handling routine waste?**

   a. Goggles.

   b. A mask.

   c. A sweatshirt.

   d. Gloves.

3 **What should you do before collecting routine waste?**

   a. Make sure your colleagues are on site.

   b. Wear your PPE.

   c. Secure all bags.

   d. Check that collection vehicles are on site.

4 **Why is it important to check the weight of a bag before disposing it?**

   a. So that the contents won't burst.

   b. There may be something valuable inside.

   c. You may be injured if it is very heavy to lift.

   d. It will indicate the origin of the waste.

5 **Which of the following should not be recycled in the workplace?**

   a. Plastic.

   b. Glass.

   c. Paper.

   d. Chemicals.

6 **If you discover a suspicious package what should you do first?**

   a. Secure the area and contact the supervisor.

   b. Remove the package to a safe place.

   c. Open the package to see what is inside.

   d. Evacuate the building and contact the police.

7 **Why is it important to maintain personal hygiene when handling waste?**

   a. So that you look tidy.

   b. To prevent cross-contamination.

   c. The company has told you to.

   d. It reduces complaints.

8 **What is the most important reason that storage areas should be kept free from waste?**

   a. It helps to reduce smells.

   b. It gives clearer access.

   c. To prevent and control pest infestation.

   d. To separate recycled waste.

Chapter 4

Dealing with routine and non-routine waste

9 **What should you do if you notice a waste container is damaged?**

a. Put out a notice to warn everyone.

b. Don't say anything as it is not important.

c. Report it to your supervisor.

d. Use it carefully.

10 **If you see a large waste spillage what should you do?**

a. Report it to your supervisor.

b. Hope that it will get washed away with the rain.

c. Tell members of the public.

d. Not worry as it is not your job to clean it up.

11 **You should always wash your hands after:**

a. going to the toilet.

b. taking medication.

c. using a telephone.

d. All of the above.

12 **Waste should be controlled to:**

a. comply with regulations.

b. avoid accidents.

c. prevent cross-contamination.

d. All of the above.

13 **A sure sign of pest infestation is:**

a. ripped waste bags.

b. mouse droppings.

c. flies.

d. a strange smell.

14 **Cleaning and relining waste collection bins is important because:**

a. it will eliminate bad smells.

b. it prevents risk of infection.

c. it avoids attracting pests.

d. All of the above.

15 **Detergents and chemicals are:**

a. sometimes recycled.

b. always recycled.

c. never recycled.

d. recycled once a year.

Dealing with non-routine waste.

16 **Why is it important to put out warning signs when collecting waste?**

a. So that everyone can see you are busy.

b. To prevent injury to others.

c. Because it shows other people that you are doing an important job.

d. So that your supervisor knows where you are.

17 **Which is the best way to transfer non-routine waste?**

a. Put it in a cardboard box.

b. Fill the container as full as possible.

c. Put it in a selected container.

d. Use a black bag.

18 **How would you identify non-routine waste?**

a. The bag is coloured.

b. The bag is labelled.

c. The bag is thick.

d. The waste is in a cardboard box.

19 What is the most important reason to dispose of non-routine waste correctly?

a. It saves costs to the company.

b. To recycle and save the environment.

c. To avoid cross-contamination and infection.

d. To keep clean.

20 How would you safely dispose of sharps?

a. Put out warning signs.

b. Place in a plastic bag.

c. Pick up and wrap in thick cardboard.

d. Use collection tweezers or tongs and place in clinical waste container.

21 How should clinical waste be disposed of?

a. By recycling.

b. Put in a general waste container.

c. By incineration.

d. Ask your supervisor.

22 When separating and sorting waste for recycling, which would you do first?

a. Make sure everywhere is clean and tidy.

b. Separate glass and cans.

c. Separate paper and card.

d. Wear the correct protective clothing.

23 How would you dispose of waste from a sanitation bin?

a. Put it in a bag with other waste.

b. Label it and incinerate.

c. Recycle it.

d. Leave it for someone else to dispose of.

24 What is the most important reason to keep waste storage areas clean?

a. Reduce smells.

b. Prevent and control pests and vermin.

c. Improve the environment.

d. Prevent injury.

25 Where should a waste holding area be located?

a. As far away as possible from the building.

b. Where there is easy and safe access.

c. In an area that is difficult to find.

d. As close as possible to food areas.

26 In what colour bag should you dispose of clinical waste?

a. Black.

b. Red.

c. It doesn't matter what colour.

d. Yellow.

27 How long should Waste Transfer Notes be retained for?

a. Six months.

b. Three years.

c. Ten years.

d. One week.

28 A hypodermic needle should be disposed of in a:

a. yellow bag.

b. black bag.

c. sharps bin.

d. recycling bin.

Chapter 5

Cleaning internal surfaces and areas

CLEANING IN PROGRESS

What you will learn:

- General considerations in cleaning
- Cleaning and maintaining internal surfaces
- Planning the sequence of cleaning
- Cleaning and maintaining floors
- Storing your equipment and finishing the work

Personal hygiene

Your aim is to contribute to the hygiene of the area in which you work. So the way you look and your personal cleanliness are important.

You would not appear to be a good cleaner if you were not concerned about your own appearance. You should bear in mind the following points regarding your appearance and personal hygiene.

- If your company has provided you with a uniform, you must wear it.
- Wear all the personal protective equipment (PPE) provided for you, such as gloves, tabard, plastic apron.
- All your work clothes must be kept clean and ironed.
- Keep yourself clean as well, and tidy and tie your hair back if required.
- Maintain personal hygiene.
- Wash your hands regularly.

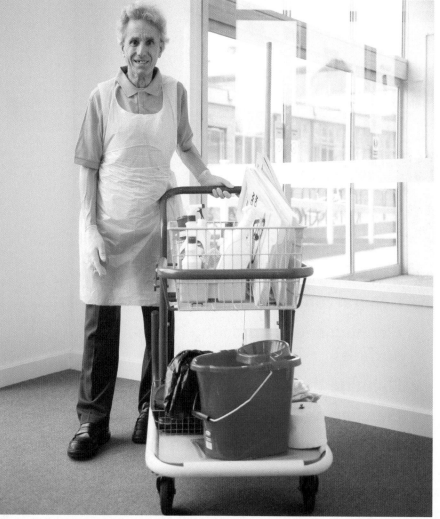

All cleaning personnel should wear clean PPE.

Security of the premises

It is important that you follow your company's procedures (see Health and safety for the cleaning and support services industry, page 3) when entering and leaving the premises. If your workplace is not your company's premises you may also need to check the customer's procedures, as they could be different from those of your company.

You need to be aware of the security procedures such as signing in and out, or clocking in and out. This is important in case of a fire and provides a record of who is on the premises.

You may be responsible for keys or setting alarms. So you should also know how to secure the building and how to operate security equipment. Always be aware of your responsibilities with regard to security.

Figure 5.1. Be aware of the security procedures in your workplace.

It is also important that you are aware of what you need to do if you come across an unattended or suspicious package (see Dealing with routine and non-routine waste, page 94), or any lost property. This is because an unclaimed package could be a danger to yourself and others. Also lost property can be returned to its owner quickly if you follow the procedures.

TASK

☐ What permits and checks are required for you to work on the premises of your company or workplace?

_____

_____

☐ Why is it important that you follow security procedures?

_____

_____

☐ What could happen if you did not follow the correct security procedures?

_____

_____

Internal surfaces (such as furniture and fixtures, doors, walls and flooring) collect dust, germs (such as **bacteria**) and dirt, which builds up over time. Regular cleaning of these surfaces helps to prevent the spread of disease and infection. It also provides a pleasant environment.

Preparing for cleaning internal surfaces

Before you begin to clean inside a premises, you must be prepared to get the task done quickly and efficiently.

So first of all you need to know what surfaces you are going to clean. These could include:

- furniture and fittings
- walls, doors and partitions
- glass surfaces and mirrors
- hard and soft floor surfaces.

Once you have inspected the area to be cleaned you will need to assemble the cleaning agents and equipment that you require from your storeroom.

Your **work schedule** should tell you what your cleaning duties are for the area you are responsible for. It should list the tasks and the equipment that you will need. If you follow your **method statement** carefully you will always perform your cleaning to the required standard as specified in your **job description**. Make sure that your storeroom is kept tidy, so that you can find what you need and ensure that it is in good condition.

> **DEFINITION**
>
> **Bacteria**
>
> Bacteria are germs that are present everywhere, some of which can cause diseases in humans. Bacteria are very tiny, so they can only be seen under a microscope.

> **DEFINITIONS**
>
> **Job description**
>
> This is a list of tasks that you cover over a period of time
>
> **Work schedule**
>
> A list of jobs you need to complete on a given day. It usually has a timeline.
>
> **Method statement**
>
> A method statement describes how to complete an individual task on the work schedule with a list of equipment and materials.

Cleaning and maintaining internal surfaces

Figure 5.2. Keeping storerooms tidy aids preparation.

TASK

Have a look in your storeroom. Make a list of the cleaning agents and equipment you keep there.

_____

_____

_____

☐ Why is it important that you keep your storeroom clean and tidy?

_____

_____

☐ Why should you keep your storeroom locked?

_____

_____

TASK

Find the work schedule for the area that you clean.

☐ What different types of areas are you required to clean?

_____

_____

☐ Why is it important that you follow your work schedule?

_____

_____

☐ What should you do if you cannot find the equipment and materials you require in your storeroom?

_____

_____

Using the correct cleaning equipment

You may have to adapt your cleaning method according to the materials and equipment that you have available. Remember the following rules:

- Inspect the surface to be cleaned and the amount and type of dirt.

- Always wear the PPE provided for you and recommended by the manufacturer, e.g. protective gloves and aprons.

- Always read the manufacturer's instructions and follow them.

- Consider the environment. **Microfibre** methods may not require the use of cleaning agents.

- Test the surface you wish to clean with the product in an area that is not so noticeable to make sure it does not cause damage.

- Check the dilution rates. If your solution is too weak it will not do the job. If it is too strong, it may cause damage.

- Chemicals should not be mixed. Chlorine and acid-based cleaners, such as toilet cleaners, will produce a dangerous gas if mixed. Mixing any acid cleaner with an alkaline cleaner will cause inactivation. This means they cancel each other out and become ineffective.

Cleaning and maintaining internal surfaces

If you do not have the materials and equipment that you require, you must inform your supervisor, or check the manufacturer's instructions before using an alternative product.

*Figure 5.3.
Mixing cleaning
agents is dangerous.*

Types of cleaning products

There are many different methods of cleaning and products available to choose from. Some that you might come across are described here.

Cleaning cloths

Whatever the type of surface you are cleaning, you will need to use a cloth. These may be disposable or re-usable. It is essential that you select the correct colour-coded cloth for the area that you are cleaning. If you mix up your cloths you could spread germs throughout the building by cross-contamination (see Health, safety and security, page 6–7).

Microfibre cleaning

Microfibre methods of cleaning may not require the use of cleaning products. The microfibres act like a magnet to attract the dirt and draw it into the cloth. A microfibre cloth can be used wet or dry. Follow these steps for their use:

1. Fold the cloth into quarters.

2. Place a flat hand on the cloth and wipe.

3. When the surface of the cloth becomes dirty, re-fold the cloth to use a clean surface.

4. When all the surfaces are dirty, use another cloth.

> **DEFINITION**
>
> **Microfibres**
>
> Microfibres are very thin, artificial (synthetic) fibres that are used to make microfibre cleaning cloths. The fibres themselves are made from materials such as polyesters, polyamides (nylon), or a mix of the two. Cloth made from microfibres will have different softness, durability and ability to absorb water, depending on the type of microfibre used to make it. Microfibre methods of cleaning do not always require the use of cleaning products. The microfibres in the material act like a magnet and attract the dust, drawing it into the cloth. If a cleaning product is required the manufacturer will recommend which products may be used and when they should be used.

Cleaning and maintaining internal surfaces

If a cleaning product is required, you should read the manufacturer's instructions on both the cloth and the cleaning product to check if it should be applied to the cloth or the surface. Always ask your supervisor if you are unsure. Microfibre cloths must be washed at 60 degrees for at least ten minutes. However, always follow the manufacturer's recommendations.

Alkaline cleaning materials are usually used for cleaning **organic matter**. **Acidic cleaning materials** are used for cleaning **non-organic** matter.

The pH of a substance tells you how acidic or alkaline a substance is. This is important to know because the amount of acidity or alkalinity determines how effective the cleaning agent will be for a selected task.

The pH is represented by a number ranging from 0 to 14. Distilled water, which is pure water, has a pH of 7, which means it is neutral (that is, neither acidic nor alkaline).

In chemistry, pH 7 is the only neutral point on the pH scale. Anything with pH less than 7 is acidic and more than 7 is alkaline. But in terms of commercial products, materials with a pH of between 6 and 9 are considered neutral.

- Alkaline materials usually have a pH within the range 9 to 13.

- Caustic materials have a pH above 13 (although 'alkaline' is used to describe substances that have a pH higher than 7, caustic substances are those alkaline substances that will burn or destroy living tissue).

- Acidic materials usually have a pH within the range 0 to 5.

For a given product, the strength of the solution you make will affect its pH. For every complete point on the scale, the strength of the solution increases by 10. In other words, a product with a pH of 9 is ten times more alkaline than a product with a pH of 8.

0	7	14
acid	neutral	alkali

Figure 5.4. The pH scale

To test whether a solution is acidic or alkaline you can use litmus or universal indicator paper. Follow the instructions supplied with the paper for doing the test correctly.

Cleaning products used in the cleaning of washrooms

Neutral detergents

Neutral detergents (pH 6–9) are also called general-purpose detergents. As the name suggests these detergents are used for all routine cleaning. Approximately 80 per cent of micro-organisms can be removed from surfaces using a neutral detergent.

You should follow the manufacturer's instructions when using a neutral detergent. This is because if too much is used, the detergent may leave the surface sticky. A sticky surface is likely to retain or attract more dust.

Acid cleaners

The main materials used in the manufacture of acid cleaners are substances which are made from phosphoric acid, sodium bisulphate, oxalic acid, hydrochloric acid and sulphuric acid. Nitric acid can damage stainless steel if not diluted correctly. It is imperative that manufacturer's instructions are followed to avoid damaging surfaces.

Acid cleaners are usually diluted. You should measure the amounts carefully to avoid damaging the surfaces on which cleaners are used.

Acid cleaners are used mainly to remove non-organic material from surfaces, for example **limescale** from toilet bowls.

Alkaline detergents

Alkaline detergents are used for cleaning things that require a strong detergent to clean them. Examples are: hard surfaces, carbon black marks, a lot of dirt, very dirty walls and paintwork.

> **Hard surface cleaners** Hard surface cleaners usually have a pH of 9 to 11. They are used for cleaning surfaces with heavy soilage, for example heavily impacted dirt or grease.

Glass cleaning products

Glass cleaning products are usually solutions made by dissolving chemicals in water. Some products have a very fine abrasive added to the solution.

Cleaning and maintaining internal surfaces

Disinfectants

Usually you should not need to use chemical disinfectants for cleaning purposes.

The problems associated with using chemical disinfectants are:

- For **disinfection** to be effective, the surface first has to be cleaned to remove all traces of organic matter.

- No single disinfectant works against all the germs that could be present. So a variety of disinfectants are required to ensure surfaces are clear of germs.

- You need to leave a disinfectant in contact with the surface being cleaned for some time for it to be effective. This could be up to 30 minutes. During the contact time of the disinfectant the surface will need to be kept wet with the disinfectant solution. Sometimes the solution needs to be kept at a particular temperature too.

- How much you dilute a disinfectant is important for it to work. If too strong a solution is used it may damage the surface. If it is too weak it may not work against the germs.

- Once diluted, disinfectants start to spoil. This means they lose their ability to work effectively against germs.

- It is important to keep clean the containers and equipment used in the dilution and for storage of disinfectants. Otherwise germs will grow in or on them, which will cause the disinfectant to become ineffective.

Figure 5.5. There are different types of cleaning products you can use.

Planning the sequence of cleaning

The simple rule you must follow is:

DO THINGS IN THE RIGHT ORDER!

Doing things in the wrong order doesn't make much sense – you wouldn't mop the floor before cleaning the tables would you? Sometimes it can be hard to decide the order of cleaning. But if you do things in the wrong order you might as well not do them at all. Doing things in the wrong order means that you will be moving the dust and dirt around instead of removing it.

You may need to:

- check with other people working in the area that it is convenient for you to clean at that time – you may need to inform them of how long you will take.

Figure 5.6. Work schedules are important and help you work effectively.

- **ventilate** the area to avoid the build up of fumes from any products being used and to aid the drying process.

- look at the area and decide what equipment and materials you need.

- gather together everything you need and take it to the area you are working in. This will save you time and help you to work more efficiently. If there are any consumable items that need replenishing ensure you take these to your work area.

Some general rules to remember are:

- Put out your warning signs and ventilate the area.

- Remove obstacles before you start to clean.

- Carry out any dust-making tasks before cleaning surfaces.

- Remove loose dust and **debris** from surfaces.

- Work from high levels to low levels when dry dusting, except when wall washing.

- Clean from 'clean areas' to 'dirty areas' so that you do not transfer dirt from dirty to clean areas.

> ### DEFINITIONS
>
> **Ventilation**
>
> Ventilation is the process of letting air into an area to ensure a constant supply of fresh air.
>
> **Debris**
>
> Debris consists of dust and waste matter.

Planning the sequence of cleaning

- Always keep your cleaning equipment out of the way of users of the building so that it does not cause an obstruction.

- Ensure that power leads do not cause a tripping hazard.

- Always check the quality of your work as you go along.

TASK

Look at your work schedule and pick one of the types of areas that you clean; e.g. offices, corridors, meeting room. Write down the cleaning tasks that you carry out in that area in the order that you carry them out.

1 _____

2 _____

3 _____

4 _____

5 _____

Now that you have prepared correctly, let's have a look at the **STEPS** involved in the cleaning process in detail one at a time.

Step one

Empty the waste bins. This job creates dust, so that is why it has to be done first. Check that the bin is clean before you re-line it.

If you need to dry mop the floor, do so now, as sweeping creates dust. If you are going to vacuum clean, or dust control mop, just pick up any debris at this stage that may block or damage your vacuum cleaner.

Step two

Start by cleaning the high level surfaces. This makes more sense than starting from the bottom and working upwards, as the dust will fall down as you clean. Use a static or microfibre duster or a vacuum cleaner with the correct attachment to remove the dust from high surfaces.

Planning the sequence of cleaning

Step three

Next move to the centre level of the room and spend some time here. This is the level that everyone looks at. Inspect the surfaces to be cleaned and remove any loose dust using a microfibre or **static duster**.

Always work from the cleanest to the dirtiest surfaces to avoid spreading the dirt. If you were cleaning an untidy desk, for example, start at the left hand corner and lift the items on the desk, dust underneath them and put them down. Work to the right hand corner until the whole desk has been cleaned. If the desk is covered in papers, you may be asked not to clean it.

After the initial dry cleaning of surfaces you will be able to see any stains clearly. So now you can start to damp dust. Make sure that you use the correct cleaning methods and agents for the surfaces that you are cleaning.

> **DEFINITION**
>
> **Static duster**
>
> The fibres in a static duster attract and hold the dust, preventing it from scattering and being re-circulated.

Step four

If you are using a microfibre cloth, keep it damp and keep re-folding to ensure that you are using a clean surface. If you are using a colour-coded cloth and bucket to damp dust, make sure that your bucket is only half full of hand-hot water and the correct amount of detergent. (Hot water is more effective at removing dust and grease. However, the water should not be too hot as you have to put your hand into it with gloves.) Rinse your cloth frequently and wring it out well. Change the water in the bucket as it becomes dirty. Take care not to use too much water on wooden surfaces as it may cause damage.

If you are using a spray polish, read the manufacturer's instructions for the cloth and spray polish to check if it should be sprayed onto the cloth or furniture. If you are unsure always check with your supervisor.

Always make sure that surfaces are dry and free from smears when you have finished cleaning. Do this by polishing dry with your microfibre cloth, disposable cloth or dry paper roll. Remember that germs may breed in surfaces that are left damp.

Clean any glass surfaces. Before cleaning the glass you may have to use a scraper/abrasive pad carefully to remove any sticky substances or paint. Use the cleaning product according to the manufacturer's instructions or dilute detergent correctly. Use a colour-coded or microfibre cloth to systematically clean and remove grease and dirt. Finally buff to a shine and remove smears.

Ensure that all surrounding areas, frames and sills, are also left clean and dry.

Step five

Now look around at the lower levels and follow the same procedures to clean underneath furniture, the skirting, the pipework and into any corners not covered by furniture. Don't ignore any awkward places. Tell your supervisor if you cannot remove any stains, or if there are any cleaning problems that you do not have the skills to carry out.

Step six

Check any consumable items, e.g. paper towels, have been replenished and adequate supplies left. Always ensure that any items that you have moved for cleaning purposes have been returned to their original positions.

Step seven

The final step will be to clean the floor. This is covered in detail in the next section as the method of cleaning will vary according to the floor type.

Cleaning and maintaining floors

Different types of floors require different cleaning procedures.

Different types of floor surface can be divided as follows:

- Hard floors – quarry tiles, ceramic tiles, concrete, terrazzo

- Semi-hard – wood, vinyl, altro, rubber, cork

- Soft – carpet, carpet tiles, rugs

Selecting the correct cleaning agent and equipment to clean floors

You may need to select equipment from the following list:

- vacuum cleaner

- sweeping brush or mop sweeper

- dustpan and brush

- microfibre mop and bucket

- colour-coded mop bucket and mop

- neutral detergent or hard surface cleaner

- warning signs.

Figure 5.7. It is vital that warning signs are in place when cleaning floors.

TASK

Look at the different types of floor surface that you have to clean. What methods and equipment do you use for each type?

Floor	Type	Equipment	Cleaning agent	Dilution rate

Preparing the area where floors need to be cleaned

Move any moveable furniture, but do not move heavy items without assistance. Place your warning signs and start by removing all dust from the floor surface.

Cleaning soft floors

1   Use a vacuum cleaner. Check the cable and plug to make sure that it is safe to use. Check the vacuum bag is not full.

2   Work with the cable behind you and clean right up to the skirting boards. Work systematically starting at the furthest point from the exit.

3   Ensure that the cable does not trail and cause a danger to others.

4   Use the correct attachment to clean into corners.

5   Make sure that the dust bag is emptied regularly into the correct refuse sack and disposed of correctly.

6   Clean and store your vacuum correctly, wiping the outside and the cable with a damp cloth as you wind the cable to replace it.

Cleaning semi-hard and hard floors

1 Use a vacuum cleaner if possible, but not if the floor is wet.

2 If a vacuum cleaner cannot be used then you may use a **dust control mop** or sweep the floor. Remember that if you sweep the floor, some of the dust will be re-circulated, so you can collect the dust more effectively if you use a dust control mop. Keep the mop's head in contact with the floor at all times.

3 Collect the debris using a dustpan and brush and dispose of correctly into a refuse bag.

> **DEFINITION**
>
> **Dust control mop**
>
> A dust control mop is equipment that traps dust and prevents it re-circulating.

4 Use a colour-coded mop and bucket or microfibre mop.

5 Fill the bucket with hot clean water. If you are using a cleaning agent, add the correct amount to the water in the bucket to avoid splashing foam into the eyes.

6 Clean around the edges of the room first, up to the skirtings.

7 Then start at the furthest point from the exit and work backwards, keeping the bucket behind you.

8 Use overlapping strokes of the mop, working backwards. Rinse the mop in the mop bucket frequently and squeeze out the excess water.

9 Change the water in the bucket as required.

10 Try to leave the surface as dry as possible to prevent risk of accidents or smears.

Dealing with a known contaminated spillage

A circumstance where you may need to use disinfectant is a known contaminated spillage. In dealing with such a spillage you should follow four steps:

1. Remove the spillage using an absorption method, e.g. paper towels.

2. Clean the area with a detergent.

3. Clean the area with a hypochlorite solution.

4. Check the surface when you have finished cleaning.

It is important to choose the correct cleaning product to suit the type of surface to be cleaned and the type of soilage. The Control of Substances Hazardous to Health Regulation 2002 (COSHH; see Health, safety and security, page 15) requires an employer to, among other things:

- assess the risk (see Health, safety and security, pages 4–6)

- decide what precautions are required

- prevent or adequately control exposure to harmful chemicals

- ensure their employees are properly informed, trained and supervised while using disinfectants.

Figure 5.8. All spillages should be cleaned as quickly as possible to prevent risk of injury to yourself or others.

TASK

How would you remove the following spillages from the different floor types?

Floor type	Spillage	Method used	Equipment used
Tiled	Orange juice		
Carpet	Food crumbs		
Altro	Urine		
Entrance mat	Tea		

Chapter 5

Cleaning internal surfaces and areas

Storing your equipment and finishing the work

Always dispose of cleaning materials/equipment carefully. It may be that you will have to dispose of cloths or mop heads that are badly soiled. Follow your company's policy for correct disposal. Always clean equipment that is to be re-used and store dry to prevent germs from growing.

Remember that good cleaning starts and finishes with a clean and tidy storeroom.

So put all of your equipment away carefully.

DEFINITION

Slurry

Slurry is a dirty solution resulting from the cleaning process.

- Dispose of **slurry** down the sluice sink or down an outside drain.

- Wash any reusable cloths and mops and make sure that they are stored dry. If you are using a microfibre system of cleaning, ensure that cloths and mop heads are correctly bagged for laundering. Dispose of disposable cloths in the correct refuse bag.

- Dispose of any disposable PPE, e.g. gloves or apron. Wash re-usable gloves and store dry.

- Check that your cleaning equipment is in good order as you store it. Inform your supervisor if anything needs replacing or if you need any items of stock.

- Return all of your equipment to a safe place, e.g. a locked cupboard to avoid it falling into the wrong hands or being the cause of an accident.

You may be disobeying the law if you do not store cleaning materials correctly. See the Health and Safety at Work etc. Act and the Control of Substances Hazardous to Health Regulations (COSHH) 2002 in Health, safety and security, page 15.

Any problems that you have encountered when carrying out your cleaning tasks should be reported to your supervisor.

Storing your equipment and finishing the work

These problems might include the following:

- broken fixtures and fittings that need maintenance
- stains that you have been unable to remove from surfaces
- any accidental damage that may have been caused by the cleaning process
- any rooms that you have been unable to gain access to.

On completion of your cleaning always check your work is of a high standard. Ensure that everywhere has been left clean and dry and meets the requirements of the area.

Figure 5.9. When you have finished make sure everywhere has been left clean and tidy.

Knowledge test

1   **What permits or checks are required for you to work on the premises? Select all that apply.**

   a. A clean driver's licence.

   b. A Criminal Records Bureau check.

   c. A reference from a previous employer.

   d. An identity badge.

2   **Why is it important to follow the correct procedures when entering or leaving your workplace? Select all correct answers.**

   a. To prevent unauthorised people entering the premises.

   b. So your Employer knows if you are late for work.

   c. To prevent possible theft or damage to property.

   d. So that your Employer knows that you are on the premises.

3   **Why is it important to be clean and tidy at work? Select two answers.**

   a. So that you are ready to go out after work.

   b. To ensure a high standard of hygiene.

   c. To prevent the spread of germs.

   d. So that you do not hurt yourself while at work.

4   **Why is it important that you have the skill and knowledge to perform the cleaning tasks you are required to complete? Select two answers.**

   a. So that you can work safely.

   b. So that you might be promoted.

   c. So that all cleaning is performed to a high standard.

   d. So that you can finish work early.

5   **What factors influence the type of cleaning method that you select? Select two answers.**

   a. The colour of the surface to be cleaned.

   b. The amount of dirt to be removed.

   c. The instructions on the container.

   d. If the cleaning product has a nice smell.

6   **How do you decide on the correct methods of cleaning each of the areas you clean? Select two answers.**

   a. You inspect the area and look at the different surfaces to be cleaned.

   b. Ask your colleague.

   c. Just use whatever you can find in the store cupboard.

   d. Read the instructions on the products in the store cupboard.

7   **Which items of personal protective equipment might you be required to wear when cleaning. Select all answers that apply.**

   a. Ear defenders.

   b. Protective gloves.

   c. Safety shoes.

   d. Protective apron.

8   **Why is it important to wear personal protective equipment and for others to see you wearing it? Select two answers.**

   a. So that you look nice at work.

   b. To create a good impression.

   c. For the security of the building.

   d. So that you can work safely for yourself and others.

9 **What information should be on a Work Schedule? Select 2 correct answers.**

   a. The names of the staff that work on the area.

   b. What cleaning tasks should be performed.

   c. The equipment and materials to use.

   d. An emergency contact number.

10 **Why do you need to use different colour-coded equipment for the areas you are required to clean?**

   a. So that the colours co-ordinate with the décor.

   b. So that you don't use too many cloths.

   c. So that you know which cloths belong to you and which belong to your colleagues.

   d. To prevent the spread of germs through cross-contamination.

11 **What factors must you consider to ensure that you clean without causing injury or damage? Select two answers.**

   a. Always mix products to get a better result.

   b. Use the same product on all surfaces.

   c. Always wear personal protective equipment.

   d. Always check the manufacturer's instructions.

12 **How do you ensure that you work to the correct time allowed for cleaning?**

   a. Wear a watch.

   b. Make sure you finish early.

   c. Ask your colleagues.

   d. Follow your work schedule.

13 **How do you know that your work is to the correct standard? Select two answers.**

   a. Ask your supervisor to check your work.

   b. Work with a colleague.

   c. Use as many products as possible.

   d. Follow your work schedule.

14 **How do you ensure that you use your equipment and materials correctly? Select two answers.**

   a. Ask your friends.

   b. Guess the dilution rate and use a 'bit extra' for a good result.

   c. Do not use anything until you have been trained how to use it.

   d. Read the manufacturer's instructions.

15 **What could happen if you used incorrect products or did not follow the manufacturer's instructions?**

   a. You will work more quickly.

   b. You will get a better result.

   c. Your supervisor will be pleased that you can use your initiative.

   d. You may cause damage to surfaces or injure yourself.

Knowledge test

16 How do you know when to change your cleaning method to suit the type of soiling and the surface you are cleaning? Select two answers.

a. Read the manufacturer's instructions on containers.

b. Check with your friends.

c. It doesn't make any difference, you just use the same product.

d. Check with your supervisor.

17 What would indicate to you that there was an infestation of pests? Select 2 answers.

a Unlocked doors.

b Droppings and carcasses.

c Damage to furniture and fittings.

d A pleasant smell.

18 How do you ensure that your cleaning causes as little disruption to the public/customer as possible?

a. Leave all your equipment out when cleaning.

b. Ensure that you carry out cleaning tasks when the building is busiest.

c. Always clean the entrance when people are arriving at work.

d. Ensure that all cleaning is scheduled to be carried out when the building is least in use.

19 Why is it important to check the quality of your work as you go along? Select two answers.

a. So that you can finish early.

b. To ensure that you have not missed any cleaning tasks.

c. To make sure that the floor is not wet.

d. To check that all cleaning has been carried out to the correct standard.

20 How do you identify and deal with tasks that are outside of your area of skill or responsibility?

a. If you are unsure, inform your supervisor and take their advice.

b. Work with a colleague.

c. Just try to do them anyway.

d. Leave any tasks that you cannot do yourself and forget about them.

21 What should you do if you cause any accidental damage while cleaning?

a. Try to put it right.

b. Just leave it and forget about it.

c. Report it to your supervisor straight away.

d. Use another product.

22 **What do you do with your equipment and materials after use?**

a. Hide them, so that no one else can find them.

b. Leave them in a corridor.

c. Return them to the storeroom to clean and store securely.

d. Leave them for someone else to clean.

23 **What do you do if you need extra or replacement resources?**

a. Tell your supervisor.

b. Tell your work colleagues.

c. Leave a note in your storeroom.

d. Leave it for someone else to sort out.

Chapter 6

Cleaning washrooms

What you will learn:

- The importance of cleaning washrooms
- Personal hygiene when cleaning washrooms
- Equipment to be used when cleaning washrooms
- Cleaning methods to be used when cleaning washrooms

The importance of cleaning washrooms

The term 'washrooms' covers a range of facilities that includes toilets, bidets, toilet cubicles, sinks and surrounds, baths and showers, floors and walls, and waste containers.

According to the Workplace (Health, Safety and Welfare) Regulations (see Health, safety and security, page 21) your company and its customers need to ensure that toilets and washing facilities are clean, ventilated and well lit.

As part of your company's cleaning staff, it is your responsibility to ensure that rules and regulations are followed correctly at your workplace. You also need to ensure that the cleaning of these areas is carried out safely and effectively.

Cleaning of washrooms is important for two reasons:

- So that the washrooms look clean and attractive

- So that the growth of **micro-organisms** that live in these areas is kept at an acceptable level. In washrooms, the micro-organisms that we are mainly concerned about are called bacteria.

Most bacteria are harmless. Some of them are very useful to humans, for example bacteria are used to make yoghurt.

> **DEFINITION**
>
> **Micro-organisms**
>
> Micro-organisms are organisms that are too small for the human eye to see. These can be germs and bacteria.

However, some bacteria can be harmful to humans as they could cause an infection.

Bacteria will grow when:

- they are left in place for enough time – in suitable conditions bacteria will grow in number by dividing every ten to 20 minutes

- there is enough moisture – bacteria require moisture to remain alive

- there is enough food for them – bacteria require similar nutrients to humans

- there is enough warmth – bacteria grow at temperatures between 5 degrees Celsius and 63 degrees Celsius. At temperatures below and above these most bacteria will die.

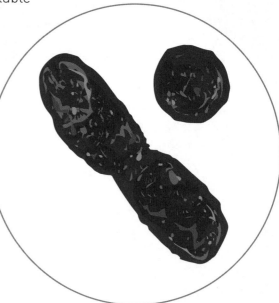

Figure 6.1. Bacteria divide quickly when the conditions are suitable.

The importance of cleaning washrooms

TASK

■ Why is important that surfaces should be left dry on completion of cleaning?

_____

_____

_____

TASK

■ Why should waste outlets and overflows be left free from dirt, hair and debris?

_____

_____

There are four main methods by which germs are passed on between places and people. These methods are:

● Through the air – some bacteria can attach themselves to tiny particles (such as dust particles). They can then be carried across large areas by the movement of air through a building.

● Contact with contaminated (polluted) matter – surfaces can be polluted with germs because of poor personal hygiene practice, such as not washing your hands after touching dirty door handles.

● Direct contact between people – for example by shaking hands.

● Through insects and animals, particularly mice, ants and flies.

Personal hygiene when cleaning washrooms

The main aim of cleaning washrooms is to remove bacteria in the area and ensure surfaces are left in a state that does not encourage further bacterial growth. Some bacteria may be harmful to human beings (see previous section). So it is important that those cleaning washrooms have good personal hygiene themselves. A member of the cleaning staff whose personal hygiene is not up to the required standard may cause contamination of areas that have already been cleaned.

You also need to be aware that as the person cleaning the washroom, you are also representing your company at your workplace.

TASK

☐ Describe the uniform provided to you by your company.

_____

_____

☐ How should you look after your uniform to ensure that you present a professional image of your company to the customer or to the public?

_____

_____

TASK

☐ When you have completed the cleaning of the washroom and returned everything to the storage area what should you do?

_____

_____

_____

Personal hygiene when cleaning washrooms

The Personal Protective Equipment at Work Regulations 1999 require that:

○ all employers should provide personal protective equipment (PPE) (see Health, safety and security, page 8) for their staff wherever there is a risk to health and safety that cannot be controlled in other ways, for example using a less powerful cleaning agent

○ if you are provided PPE you must use it at work.

TASK

▢ Usually PPE is supplied for the cleaning of washrooms. What PPE items may be supplied for the cleaning of washrooms?

_____

_____

_____

The aim of using PPE when cleaning washrooms is to:

○ protect you and your clothing from damage from chemicals

○ avoid cross-contamination (see Health, safety and security, page 6) from the washroom to you.

○ reduce the chance that you will cross-contaminate other areas once you have removed the PPE.

TASK

▢ Identify the correct PPE for cleaning washrooms, to reduce the opportunity of cross-contamination.

_____

_____

Equipment to be used when cleaning washrooms

Colour coding of equipment allows for the identification of what equipment is used where, i.e. a mop that is used to mop a toilet floor will not be used to mop a kitchen floor. So the use of colour-coded equipment helps to reduce cross-contamination.

Currently, there is no national colour-coding scheme in the UK. So your company may have its own system or use a system used by a group of companies.

The colour coding scheme that is adopted by a company or a group of companies should apply to every item used to clean a particular area, for example mops, buckets, cloths and brushes.

Figure 6.2. Colour coding indicates which equipment should be used when cleaning a particular area.

TASK

☐ Describe the colour-coding scheme that is used in your company.

_____

_____

☐ What may happen if you do not use the correct colour-coded equipment?

_____

_____

Cleaning materials to be used when cleaning washrooms

Alkaline cleaning materials are usually used for cleaning **organic matter**. **Acidic cleaning materials** are used for cleaning **non-organic** matter.

The pH of a substance tells you how acidic or alkaline a substance is. This is important to know because the amount of acidity or alkalinity determines how effective the cleaning agent will be for a selected task.

The pH is represented by a number ranging from 0 to 14. Distilled water, which is pure water, has a pH of 7, which means it is neutral (that is, neither acidic nor alkaline).

In chemistry, pH 7 is the only neutral point on the pH scale. Anything with pH less than 7 is acidic and more than 7 is alkaline. But in terms of commercial products, materials with a pH of between 6 and 9 are considered neutral.

- Alkaline materials usually have a pH within the range 9 to 13.

- Caustic materials have a pH above 13 (although 'alkaline' is used to describe substances that have a pH higher than 7, caustic substances are those alkaline substances that will burn or destroy living tissue).

- Acidic materials usually have a pH within the range 0 to 5.

DEFINITIONS

Organic matter

Organic matter is matter that comes from living or once living but now dead organisms. Examples include fingerprints, bodily waste, blood.

Non-organic matter

Non-organic matter is matter that comes from a non-living source, for example limescale, which is found in areas with hard water.

Acidic cleaning material

Acidic solutions have a pH of less than 7.

Alkaline cleaning material

Alkaline solutions have a pH of more than 7.

Chapter 6

Cleaning washrooms

For a given product, the strength of the solution you make will affect its pH. For every complete point on the scale, the strength of the solution increases by 10. In other words, a product with a pH of 9 is ten times more alkaline than a product with a pH of 8.

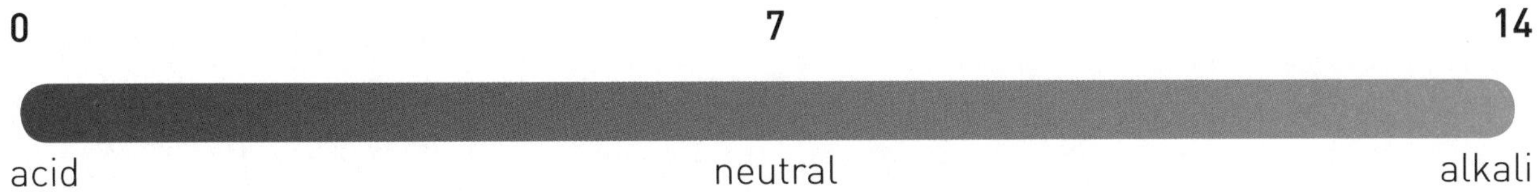

0　　　　　　　　　　　　　　　　7　　　　　　　　　　　　　　　　14

acid　　　　　　　　　　　　　neutral　　　　　　　　　　　　　alkali

Figure 6.3. The pH scale

To test whether a solution is acidic or alkaline you can use litmus or universal indicator paper. Follow the instructions supplied with the paper for doing the test correctly.

Equipment to be used when cleaning washrooms

Chemicals should not be mixed. Chlorine and acid-based cleaners, such as toilet cleaners, will produce a dangerous gas if mixed. Mixing any acid cleaner with an alkaline cleaner will cause inactivation. This means they cancel each other out and become ineffective.

TASK

Name two cleaning products used by your company for the cleaning of washrooms.

Cleaning product	Usage

Cleaning products used in the cleaning of washrooms

Neutral detergents

Neutral detergents (pH 6–9) are also called general-purpose detergents. As the name suggests these detergents are used for all routine cleaning. Approximately 80 per cent of micro-organisms can be removed from surfaces using a neutral detergent.

You should follow the manufacturer's instructions when using a neutral detergent. This is because if too much is used, the detergent may leave the surface sticky. A sticky surface is likely to retain or attract more dust.

Acid cleaners

The main materials used in the manufacture of acid cleaners are substances which are made from phosphoric acid, sodium bisulphate, oxalic acid, hydrochloric acid and sulphuric acid. Nitric acid can damage stainless steel if not diluted correctly. It is imperative that manufacturers' instructions are followed to avoid damaging surfaces.

Acid cleaners are usually diluted. You should measure the amounts carefully to avoid damaging the surfaces on which cleaners are used.

Acid cleaners are used mainly to remove non-organic material from surfaces, for example **limescale** from toilet bowls.

DEFINITIONS

Limescale

Limescale is the white-coloured, chalky, hard material that collects where water resides, typically inside kettles or around taps and at the bottom of toilet bowls.

Equipment to be used when cleaning washrooms

Alkaline detergents

Alkaline detergents are used for cleaning things that require a strong detergent to clean them. Examples are: hard surfaces, carbon black marks, a lot of dirt, very dirty walls and paintwork.

> **Hard surface cleaners** Hard surface cleaners usually have a pH of 9 to 11. They are used for cleaning surfaces with heavy soilage, for example heavily impacted dirt or grease.

Glass cleaning products

Glass cleaning products are usually solutions made by dissolving chemicals in water. Some products have a very fine abrasive added to the solution.

Disinfectants

Usually you should not need to use chemical disinfectants for cleaning purposes.

The problems associated with using chemical disinfectants are:

- For **disinfection** to be effective, the surface first has to be cleaned to remove all traces of organic matter.

- No single disinfectant works against all the germs that could be present. So a variety of disinfectants are required to ensure surfaces are clear of germs.

> **DEFINITION**
>
> **Disinfection**
>
> Disinfection either reduces or destroys the ability of germs to grow. Disinfection can be carried out using chemicals called **disinfectants** or sometimes just heat is used.

- You need to leave a disinfectant in contact with the surface being cleaned for some time for it to be effective. This could be up to 30 minutes. During the contact time of the disinfectant the surface will need to be kept wet with the disinfectant solution. Sometimes the solution needs to be kept at a particular temperature too.

- How much you dilute a disinfectant is important for it to work. If too strong a solution is used it may damage the surface. If it is too weak it may not work against the germs.

- Once diluted, disinfectants start to spoil. This means they lose their ability to work effectively against germs.

- It is important to keep clean the containers and equipment used in the dilution and for storage of disinfectants. Otherwise germs will grow in or on them, which will cause the disinfectant to become ineffective.

Dealing with a known contaminated spillage

A circumstance where you may need to use disinfectant is a known contaminated spillage. In dealing with such a spillage you should follow four steps:

1. Remove the spillage using an absorption method, e.g. paper towels.

2. Clean the area with a detergent.

3. Clean the area with a hypochlorite solution.

4. Check the surface when you have finished cleaning.

It is important to choose the correct cleaning product to suit the type of surface to be cleaned and the type of soilage. The Control of Substances Hazardous to Health Regulation 2002 (COSHH; see Health and safety for the cleaning and support services industry, page 15) requires an employer to, among other things:

- assess the risk (see Health, safety and security, pages 4–6)

- decide what precautions are required

- prevent or adequately control exposure to harmful chemicals

- ensure their employees are properly informed, trained and supervised while using disinfectants.

TASK

Why is it important to follow the manufacturer's instructions when using cleaning chemicals?

_____

_____

Equipment to be used when cleaning washrooms

TASK

When you have cleaned the washroom, you should return all the equipment and materials to their storage area and store them in a clean and safe manner. Why is this important?

_____

_____

_____

TASK

Before you start to clean a washroom area, it is normal to ensure that the area is not in use. Why is this normal practice?

_____

_____

_____

Figure 6.4. Make sure that the washroom isn't in use.

TASK

☐ Does your company have any procedures for entering and leaving washroom areas?

_____

☐ If you answered 'Yes', briefly describe what they are.

_____

_____

_____

On entering a washroom to clean it, it is good practice (see Health, safety and security, page 121) to ensure the area is well ventilated. You can do this by opening windows and/or doors. This allows foul air to go out and it also speeds up the drying of surfaces after cleaning.

You must avoid cross-contamination of areas when cleaning washrooms. So always start from the clean area and clean towards the dirty area. This rule applies whether you are using a one-cloth or **colour coding system**.

DEFINITION

Colour coding system

In a multi-cloth system, within a specified area different coloured cloths are used to carry out specific tasks.

TASK

☐ Identify the order in which a washroom should be cleaned.

1 _____

2 _____

3 _____

4 _____

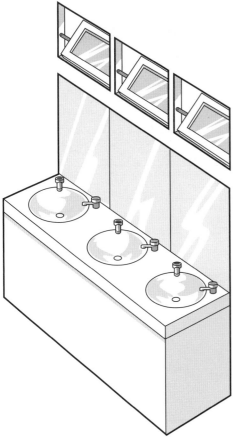

Figure 6.5. It is important that areas are ventilated.

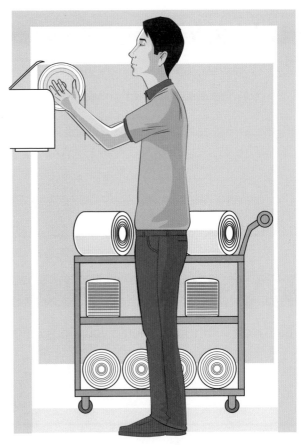

Figure 6.6. Replacing consumables is important in maintaining hygiene standards.

When dusting in washrooms you should always damp dust. This is to avoid spreading dust around the area.

You should also replace any used-up consumables (toilet rolls, soap, paper/roller towels). This is important as it means that your customers are able to ensure their own personal hygiene is maintained. It also avoids the possibility of complaints being received.

TASK

▢ When filling dispensers, why is it important to follow the manufacturer's instructions?

_____

_____

TASK

Describe your company's procedure for ensuring that you always have adequate supplies of consumables.

_____

_____

_____

TASK

How and where should you store consumables?

_____

_____

Some of the waste products you may come across when cleaning washrooms are:

- used paper towels

- **sharps**

- non-clinical waste

- clinical waste.

DEFINITION

Sharps

Sharps are instruments such as needles, syringes or blades, which could pierce your skin or PPE. This means they could potentially cause injury or pass on infection.

Cleaning methods to be used when cleaning washrooms

TASK

What is your company's policy for collection, storage and disposal of the waste products listed below?

- Non-clinical waste

  _____

  _____

- Clinical waste

  _____

  _____

- Sharps

  _____

  _____

Unfortunately, from time to time you may come across damaged or broken fixtures and fittings in washrooms.

Most companies will have a written method statement for the cleaning of washrooms. Obtain a copy of your company's method statement for the cleaning of washrooms.

Figure 6.7. All breakages and faults need to be reported.

TASK

- Describe your company's procedures for reporting faults and damage.

  _____

  _____

  _____

Cleaning methods to be used when cleaning washrooms

If your company does not have a method statement, see the example given here of what it should contain.

Example method statement for cleaning a washroom

Equipment:

- colour-coded cloths
- toilet brush
- colour-coded mopping system
- non-abrasive pad
- colour-coded dustpan and brush
- colour-coded buckets
- warning signs
- colour-coded spray bottles
- PPE
- colour-coded long-handled dry sweeper

Materials:

- neutral detergent or hard surface cleaning agent
- toilet cleaning agent

Method:

1. Put on PPE.
2. Collect and check materials and equipment.
3. Place warning signs.
4. Ventilate area.
5. If appropriate, make up a solution of cleaning chemical following the manufacturer's instructions.
6. Flush the toilet bowl and drop the water level in the bowl.
7. Apply hard surface cleaning agent, remove organic soil, agitate, flush and lower the level of water.
8. Apply the toilet cleaner to the inside of the bowl and shut lid. Check the bottle to see how long it should be left.
9. Dry sweep the floor. Remove debris.
10. Damp dust – paper towel holders, soap dispensers, etc.
11. Using the appropriate colour-coded cloth and a solution of cleaning agent; damp dust/spot clean the area of vertical surface behind the sink, starting at the bottom and working up, rinsing the cloth frequently. Clean up – rinse down.
12. Remove plug hole debris.
13. Clean the overflow.
14. Using the appropriate coloured cloth/abrasive pad and solution of cleaning agent clean and rinse the exterior of the sink, rinsing the cloth/pad frequently.

15. Using the appropriate coloured cloth/abrasive pad and solution of cleaning agent clean and rinse the interior of the sink, rinsing the cloth/pad frequently.

16. Using the appropriate coloured cloth and solution of cleaning agent, damp wipe the WC handle and toilet door handle.

17. Dry and buff up if appropriate all surfaces cleaned.

18. Using the appropriate coloured cloth, starting from the top of the cistern, damp dust surfaces from top to bottom using a solution of the appropriate cleaning agent. Pay due attention to preventing cross-contamination and use the correct cleaning materials.

19. Damp wipe the toilet seat from the lid downwards.

20. If the toilet cleaning product used for cleaning the bowl has been in contact with the bowl surfaces for the appropriate length of time, scrub the surface using the toilet brush.

21. Flush the toilet.

22. Rinse and dry the toilet brush. Pay appropriate attention to the brush holder.

23. Replace any consumables.

24. Sweep the floor to remove all dust and debris.

25. Empty the waste bin.

26. Replace the bin liner.

27. Mop the floor.

28. Dispose of all unwanted cleaning materials in the appropriate manner.

29. Wash/dispose of colour-coded cloths and mops.

30. Rinse out mop bucket/buckets and leave them to dry.

31. Return all equipment and materials to the correct secure storage area and store correctly. They should be dry and clean.

32. Wash your hands.

33. When the floor surface is dry remove the warning signs.

Key points

1. Wear the PPE supplied to you.

2. Select correct materials and equipment.

3. Place warning signs.

4. Remember the colour coding.

5. Clean from clean to dirty areas.

6. Dispose of rubbish correctly.

7. Store equipment and materials after being cleaned and dried correctly.

8. Wash your hands.

Chapter 6

Cleaning washrooms

1 **When you have completed the cleaning of a washroom what should you do?**

a. Go for your break.

b. Carry on to your next job.

c. Wash your hands.

d. Tell your supervisor.

2 **Why is it important to wear PPE when cleaning washrooms?**

a. Your supervisor demands it.

b. Your customer expects it.

c. To avoid cross-contamination.

d. To protect your own clothes.

3 **Why should you check the washroom is empty before starting to clean?**

a. For health and safety.

b. To avoid embarrassment.

c. It makes cleaning more efficient.

d. So you are not watched.

4 **Why is adequate ventilation important when cleaning washrooms?**

a. To remove chemical vapour, foul smells and to aid drying.

b. To remove chemical vapour and to aid drying.

c. To remove foul smells and to aid drying.

d. To aid drying.

5 **Why should colour-coded equipment be used when cleaning washrooms?**

a. To ensure the customer is happy.

b. To avoid cross-contamination.

c. The job method statement requires it.

d. Your supervisor has instructed it.

6 **Why should loose dust, hair and debris be removed before cleaning surfaces, fixtures and fittings?**

a. It saves rinsing cloths too frequently.

b. The number of changes of cloths is reduced.

c. It aids efficient and effective cleaning.

d. It reduces the changes of rinsing water.

7 **Why is it important to follow the manufacturer's instructions when using cleaning products?**

a. For efficiency and health and safety.

b. For efficiency and economy.

c. For economy and staff training.

d. For efficiency, economy and health and safety.

8 **Why should surfaces not be over-wetted?**

a. It may leave a smeary finish.

b. It delays the usage of the area.

c. It may damage surfaces.

d. It may lead to accidents.

9 To avoid cross-contamination what is the recommended system of cleaning?

a. Clean to dirty.

b. Dirty to clean.

c. Wash then polish.

d. Top to bottom.

10 For growth, bacteria require:

a. time, nutrients and a temperature of 5 degrees Celsius to 63 degrees Celsius.

b. time, nutrients, moisture and a temperature of 5 degrees Celsius to 63 degrees Celsius.

c. time, nutrients, moisture and a temperature of 5 degrees Celsius to 83 degrees Celsius.

d. time, nutrients, moisture and a temperature of 10 degrees Celsius to 63 degrees Celsius.

11 Why is it important to ensure that waste outlets and overflows are free of dirt?

a. To avoid bad smells.

b. It is given in the method statement.

c. It gives a good impression.

d. To discourage bacterial growth.

12 Why is it important to follow the manufacturer's instructions when replenishing consumables?

a. To ensure there is always a supply.

b. To avoid unnecessary wastage.

c. To ensure the dispenser works correctly.

d. To ensure customer satisfaction.

13 If you need to order further supplies of consumables, you should:

a. ask a colleague if you can borrow some.

b. ask your line manger or supervisor.

c. follow your company's procedures.

d. ensure what you have lasts longer.

14 Why is it important that you follow workplace procedures for disposing of waste?

a. For health and safety.

b. To please your supervisor.

c. To please your customer.

d. To avoid disposal problems.

15 Why should holding areas for waste be kept clean and tidy?

a. Requirement of the contract.

b. Waste may attract pests (vermin).

c. Image of the company.

d. Supervisor requires it.

16 Why is it important that you follow your company's procedures to report faults?

a. It has been agreed with the customer.

b. Your supervisor insists on it.

c. It is most effective way to ensure repair.

d. It ensures everyone is doing the same.

Chapter 6

Cleaning washrooms

17 Why is it important to store cleaning equipment and materials correctly?

a. It reduces the opportunity for theft.

b. It aids stock control and stock rotation.

c. It helps teamwork and efficient working.

d. It reduces health and safety hazards.

18 Why should PPE equipment be removed or replaced when leaving a washroom?

a. To avoid cross contamination.

b. It is an employer and client requirement.

c. For reasons of self and organisation image.

d. To ensure colour-coding of PPE is correct.

19 How do you dispose of used PPE?

a. Throw it in a skip.

b. Place it with general waste.

c. Send it for recycling.

d. Give it to your supervisor.

20 A pathogen is a disease producing agent such as:

a. viruses.

b. bacteria.

c. micro-organisms.

d. All of the above.

21 When cleaning a washroom it is important that which of the following equipment is correctly colour-coded?

a. Cloths.

b. Mop and bucket.

c. Brushes.

d. All equipment.

22 Why when dusting in a washroom is it advisable to damp dust?

a. To avoid spreading dust.

b. It gives a good impression.

c. It is a client requirement.

d. Supervisor's instructions.

Chapter 7

Cleaning high risk areas

What you will learn:

- What are high risk areas?
- Preparing to clean high risk areas
- Maintaining a high level of hygiene
- Different types of cleaning equipment
- How to prevent the spread of infection and cross-contamination in a high risk area
- Equipment to be used when cleaning high risk areas
- Dealing with spillage of bodily fluids
- The correct order of work
- Cleaning work schedules in hospitals

What are high risk areas?

High risk areas are places where there is a high risk of infection or contamination to people, including yourself, and the environment. Examples of high risk areas are:

- hospital wards
- operating theatres
- clinical rooms
- ambulances
- care homes
- hospices
- food areas where raw and cooked foods are prepared.

Infection is not only passed from person to person but can also be transferred to people from materials, equipment or food which has become contaminated. This is called cross-contamination (see Health and safety for the cleaning and support services industry, page 6).

The results of being infected could be complications for an already ill patient, staff becoming ill are unable to work and those they have been in contact with also becoming ill. This could result in there being a strain on hospitals.

TASK

From the seven high risk areas mentioned above, give two examples for each of how/why infection or contamination can occur.

	Example 1	Example 2
hospital wards		
operating theatres		
clinical rooms		
ambulances		
care homes		
hospices		
food areas		

Preparing to clean high risk areas

To reduce risks it is important for you to maintain a high level of hygiene (including personal cleanliness) in all situations. You should also always wear the correct personal protective clothing (PPE) that has been given to you by your company.

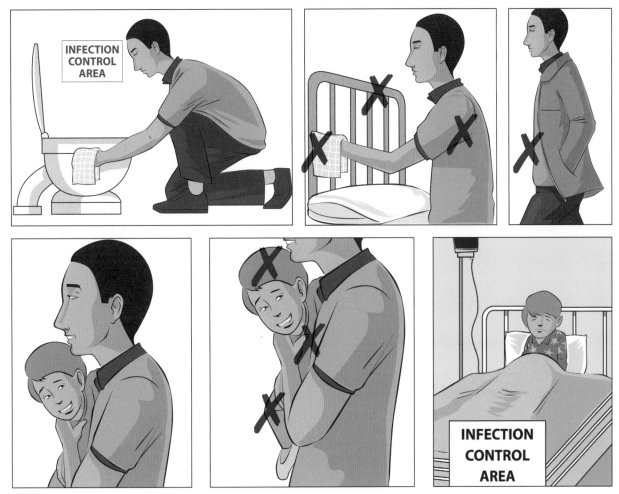

Figure 7.1. Poor hygiene can result in cross infection.

You should be thoroughly prepared so that you can carry out your cleaning duties efficiently within the time allocated to you. Preparing beforehand will enable you to consider any potential health and safety risks in your work. It will also minimise the length of time the area is out of use.

Maintaining a high level of hygiene

Before starting work, if you have a cold, or any skin problems, or any other conditions that may prevent you from doing all your cleaning duties, you should ask your supervisor for advice.

You must then change into the uniform provided for you by your employer. This should be done on your work premises, in the changing room. Remove any jewellery, your watch and mobile phone, and keep them in a safe place. Jewellery includes items such as rings, earrings, necklaces, bracelets and body piercings.

Rings should be removed before washing your hands. This is because germs can get trapped between the fingers and the ring, and they are not removed by washing your hands.

Earrings and body piercings should be removed as they may fall off and onto an area that has just been cleaned. This could cause cross-contamination. Jewellery may also get caught in machinery or equipment and cause you injury

Also remember that you will probably be using strong cleaning chemicals. If you are wearing jewellery and it does fall off or come into contact with chemicals it could be badly damaged. In such a situation, it would not be reasonable to complain to your supervisor about your loss, as you should not have been wearing it.

Mobile phones are known to contain large numbers of germs. So you would be causing cross-contamination if you were to use it while cleaning in a high risk area. It is generally unprofessional and dangerous to have a mobile phone switched on while cleaning, for all the above reasons.

You must also wear clean PPE. PPE includes disposable gloves and plastic apron, mask, goggles, overshoes and hat (see Health and safety for the cleaning and support services industry, page 8).

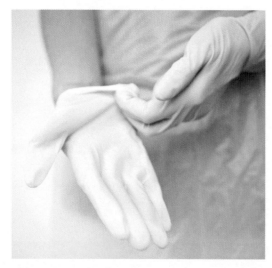

Gloves prevent infection.

Personal Protective Equipment (PPE)

Colour coded disposable gloves

Colour coded disposable gloves are worn to prevent cross-contamination from one area or item to another. In high risk areas the passing of infection could be between the patient and the cleaner. That is, the cleaner could pass on infection to the patient or the patient could pass on infection to the cleaner. So it is important that the gloves are removed and replaced with new ones when you move to cleaning a different area, for example from a washroom to a ward, when you are using different colour-coded equipment or if your gloves are torn.

Check the gloves for holes before putting on.

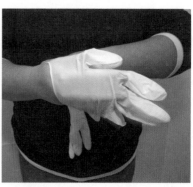

Pull the gloves on

Wearing gloves also protects your hands from cleaning chemicals. Remember you must wash your hands again before putting on the new gloves as any germs present on the old gloves will spread to the new ones.

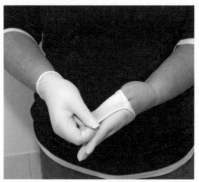

Take them off by pulling from the cuff

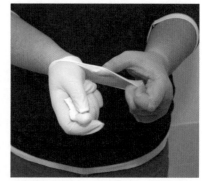

Pull off the second glove, while holding the first glove

Disposable plastic apron

A disposable plastic apron is worn to prevent cross-contamination from one area to another. It also protects your uniform from becoming contaminated with germs and cleaning chemicals. The apron should be changed and thrown away in the same situations as described for gloves. Remove your apron carefully and throw it away according to

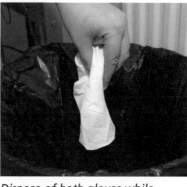

Dispose of both gloves while holding the first glove

your employer's policy (i.e. the apron should be worn for single item use). Pull to rip the neck halter and the tie bands and fold from outside in; bacteria will be the outside of the apron and care must be taken to minimise touching the outside of the apron. Hands should be washed following this activity. Aprons must be stored so that they do not gather dust that can act as a reservoir (collection place) for infection. You should follow the proper procedure for washing your hands when changing to a new apron.

Aprons help to prevent cross-contamination.

Maintaining a high level of hygiene

Mask and goggles

A mask and goggles are usually worn where there is any danger of:

- breathing in spray from a cleaning method
- your eyes being affected by strong chemicals.

You also need to wear a mask where there is a risk that you may pass on an infection to a patient who is likely to catch infections easily or is highly infectious themselves.

The gloves, apron, mask and goggles should be put on in the high risk area and taken off and disposed of appropriately before leaving the high risk area.

Overshoes

You need to wear overshoes when you are working in an area that has been cleaned, for example an operating theatre. This is to prevent germs being spread from a non-cleaned area to a cleaned one. Overshoes should be put on in the changing area provided for those going into the operating theatre and removed immediately afterwards.

Hat

You usually wear a hat to:

- prevent your hair falling into an area that has been cleaned
- protect your hair from becoming trapped in machinery
- reduce touching of hair during cleaning.

Before you wear a hat, make sure your hair is tidy and tie it back if required. Check your appearance in the mirror before leaving the changing room.

Note: At the end of your cleaning shift you should remove your uniform in the changing room and put it in the laundry bag provided before putting on your own clothes.

Hand hygiene

Good hand hygiene has been proven to lower the risk of spreading bacteria, for example **gastro-enteritis**. The virus that causes gastro-enteritis can survive in the environment for many days. Viral gastro-enteritis may be spread by several routes: faecal–oral (touching stools and then touching the mouth), by vomiting, through contaminated spray bottles, and through contaminated food and water.

Gastro-enteritis is an infection of the stomach and intestines, which can cause you to have diarrhoea, and stomach pains. You may also feel sick and vomit.

Poor hand washing is the main reason for the spread of infection to yourself and others. You should always remember to clean your hands before and after each cleaning activity.

Maintaining a high level of hygiene

This will make sure that harmful germs are not spread.

Hand washing with liquid soap is necessary after working in an area where there is an infected patient. It is also necessary after removal of your gloves and apron.

Where advised, for example where the cleaning has been carried out in an area where there is no infected patient, you can use alcohol gel if your hands are not soiled. (Alcohol does not work against some viruses so should not be used if your hands are soiled.) Alcohol gel should be located in all appropriate areas, e.g. patient bedsides, toilets, bathrooms, sinks.

> **DEFINITION**
>
> **Gastro-enteritis**
>
> Gastro-enteritis is an infection of the stomach and intestines, which can cause you to have diarrhoea, and stomach pains. You may also feel sick and vomit.

Separate protective clothing should be worn between each patient area, for example in a ward. This means that you may have to change your apron, gloves and mask many times during your cleaning shift. Otherwise you may pass germs on to other people or food.

Handling of food

If you handle food as part of your duties, take particular notice of the following:

- Let your supervisor know if you have been vomiting, or if you have diarrhoea or any sores, boils or rashes.
- Cover any cuts you have with a clean blue waterproof dressing.
- Remove your jewellery, watch and mobile phone.
- Wash your hands only in a hand-wash basin, not in a sink used for washing equipment.
- Always wash your hands after going to the toilet.
- Wash your hands after handling raw food, waste or cleaning materials.

Remember!

- Poor hand washing is the main reason for the spread of infection to yourself and others.
- Hands that are not washed properly will still have large numbers of germs on them.
- Areas that are often missed while washing hands are: the thumbs, tips of fingers, between the fingers and parts of the palm (the front of the hands).

Correct hand washing method

The pictures below show the correct hand washing method.

Stages of hand washing.

Stage 1 *Wet your hands thoroughly under running water and apply liquid soap.*

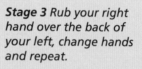

Stage 2 *Rub your hands palm to palm.*

Stage 3 *Rub your right hand over the back of your left, change hands and repeat.*

Stage 4 *Rub fingers linked to your palms.*

Stage 5 *Rotate your right hand around your left thumb, change hands and repeat.*

Stage 6 *Rotate your right hand around your left wrist, change hands and repeat.*

Stage 7 *Rinse your hands thoroughly under running water.*

Stage 8 *Dry your hands thoroughly with paper towels.*

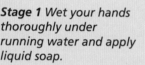

Drying your hands properly is also important as germs grow rapidly in damp conditions. Using disposable paper towels is the best way to reduce the risk of infection.

Any cuts on your hands should be covered with waterproof dressings and changed at regular intervals.

Note: You should wash your hands again after taking off your gloves to remove any bacteria that may have got on your hands while removing the gloves.

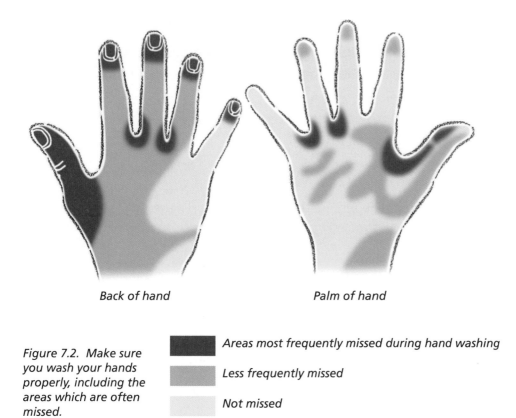

Back of hand   Palm of hand

Figure 7.2. Make sure you wash your hands properly, including the areas which are often missed.

■	*Areas most frequently missed during hand washing*
▨	*Less frequently missed*
▫	*Not missed*

TASK

▨ Before you start work, what hygiene procedures must you follow?

_____

_____

▨ Why is it important to follow these procedures?

_____

_____

▨ What could happen if you did not follow the correct procedures?

_____

_____

Different types of cleaning equipment

All equipment used should be specifically for high risk areas, colour coded or disposable. Get rid of visible soil with soap or detergent and water. Sterilisation may use steam under pressure in an autoclave, gas or radiation sterilisation (for some sensitive items). For disinfection, use the right chemicals at the correct strength. Make sure items are packaged and positioned correctly.

Cleaning cloths

Whatever surface you are cleaning, you will need to use a cloth. These may be disposable or re-usable.

Microfibre cleaning cloths

Microfibres are very thin, artificial (synthetic) fibres that are used to make microfibre cleaning cloths. The fibres themselves are made from materials such as polyesters, polyamides (nylon), or a mix of the two. Cloth made from microfibres will have different softness, durability and ability to absorb water, depending on the type of microfibre used to make it. Microfibre methods of cleaning do not always require the use of cleaning products. The microfibres in the material act like a magnet and attract the dust, drawing it into the cloth. If a cleaning product is required the manufacturer will recommend which products may be used and when they should be used.

Remember!

Before starting to clean you must wash your hands, put on your PPE, and collect the appropriate colour-coded equipment, making sure that it is in good working order.

Equipment may be coded (either labelled or colour coded) for use in different areas.

The aim of colour coding of cleaning equipment is to make sure that cross-contamination or infection does not occur when the equipment is used.

Different companies may use a different colour-coded system but the principle is the same. For example:

- red cloths, gloves, mops and buckets used only for washroom floors and toilets
- green for kitchens and food service areas
- blue for general areas
- yellow for washbasins and washrooms surfaces.

The equipment should also be marked to show which ward or area it is to be used in.

Other companies may use disposable floor pads and cloths. Check with your supervisor

Different types of cleaning equipment

which system is used in your workplace.

Always work from the cleanest area towards the dirtiest area.

There are certain risks present in high risk areas which may not occur in routine cleaning of other areas. It is important that you know how to identify these risks so that you can report them to your supervisor. Your supervisor will assess how serious the risk is and the best cleaning method to use.

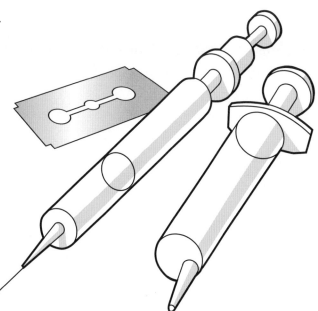

Figure 7.3. Sharps are just one of the risks in high risk areas.

TASK

■ From the following high risk areas identify one different risk for each that may be present and does not occur in routine cleaning of other areas.

	specific risk
toilets	
clinical area	
ambulance	

How to prevent the spread of infection and cross-contamination in a high risk area

Such risks could be:

- damaged items of furniture and or equipment: you should report any damaged items to your supervisor as they may contain germs. These items should be cleaned before removal from the high risk area, and before being returned to the high risk area after repair

- spillages or any soiling you are unable to identify: these may be bodily fluids

- separation of hazardous and non-hazardous waste: make sure the area has been cleared of any waste and that it has been disposed of properly. (The risk here is the hazardous waste – if it is not disposed of correctly it could cause spread of infection)

- dirty, soiled bed linen or towels: colour coded sealable bags should be used for linen contaminated with body fluids. You should not handle soiled linen and must report this to your supervisor.

Before entering a high risk area you also need to check with your supervisor which areas need particular attention. Look out for any notices, so that you are wearing the correct PPE and have with you the correct equipment and cleaning materials for the cleaning required.

Alkaline cleaning materials are usually used for cleaning **organic matter**. **Acidic cleaning materials** are used for cleaning **non-organic** matter.

The pH of a substance tells you how acidic or alkaline a substance is. This is important to know because the amount of acidity or alkalinity determines how effective the cleaning agent will be for a selected task.

The pH is represented by a number ranging from 0 to 14. Distilled water, which is pure water, has a pH of 7, which means it is neutral (that is, neither acidic nor alkaline).

In chemistry, pH 7 is the only neutral point on the pH scale. Anything with pH less than 7 is acidic and more than 7 is alkaline. But in terms of commercial products, materials with a pH of between 6 and 9 are considered neutral.

- Alkaline materials usually have a pH within the range 9 to 13.

- Caustic materials have a pH above 13 (although 'alkaline' is used to describe substances that have a pH higher than 7, caustic substances are those alkaline substances that will burn or destroy living tissue).

- Acidic materials usually have a pH within the range 0 to 5.

For a given product, the strength of the solution you make will affect its pH. For every complete point on the scale, the strength of the solution increases by 10. In other words, a product with a pH of 9 is ten times more alkaline than a product with a pH of 8.

0	7	14
acid	neutral	alkali

Figure 7.4. The pH scale

To test whether a solution is acidic or alkaline you can use litmus or universal indicator paper. Follow the instructions supplied with the paper for doing the test correctly.

Chemicals should not be mixed. Chlorine and acid-based cleaners, such as toilet cleaners, will produce a dangerous gas if mixed. Mixing any acid cleaner with an alkaline cleaner will cause inactivation. This means they cancel each other out and become ineffective.

Cleaning products used in the cleaning of washrooms

Neutral detergents

Neutral detergents (pH 6–9) are also called general-purpose detergents. As the name suggests these detergents are used for all routine cleaning. Approximately 80 per cent of micro-organisms can be removed from surfaces using a neutral detergent.

Equipment to be used when cleaning high risk areas

You should follow the manufacturer's instructions when using a neutral detergent. This is because if too much is used, the detergent may leave the surface sticky. A sticky surface is likely to retain or attract more dust.

Acid cleaners

The main materials used in the manufacture of acid cleaners are substances which are made from phosphoric acid, sodium bisulphate, oxalic acid, hydrochloric acid and sulphuric acid. Nitric acid can damage stainless steel if not diluted correctly. It is imperative that manufacturers' instructions are followed to avoid damaging surfaces.

Acid cleaners are usually diluted. You should measure the amounts carefully to avoid damaging the surfaces on which cleaners are used.

Acid cleaners are used mainly to remove non-organic material from surfaces, for example **limescale** from toilet bowls.

Alkaline detergents

Alkaline detergents are used for cleaning things that require a strong detergent to clean them. Examples are: hard surfaces, carbon black marks, a lot of dirt, very dirty walls and paintwork.

> **Hard surface cleaners** Hard surface cleaners usually have a pH of 9 to 11. They are used for cleaning surfaces with heavy soilage, for example heavily impacted dirt or grease.

Glass cleaning products

Glass cleaning products are usually solutions made by dissolving chemicals in water. Some products have a very fine abrasive added to the solution.

Disinfectants

Usually you should not need to use chemical disinfectants for cleaning purposes.

The problems associated with using chemical disinfectants are:

- For **disinfection** to be effective, the surface first has to be cleaned to remove all traces of organic matter.

- No single disinfectant works against all the germs that could be present. So a variety of disinfectants are required to ensure surfaces are clear of germs.

- You need to leave a disinfectant in contact with the surface being cleaned for some time for it to be effective. This could be up to 30 minutes. During the contact time of the disinfectant the surface will need to be kept wet with the disinfectant solution.

Equipment to be used when cleaning high risk areas

Toilet cleaners have a high acid content to remove limescale.

Sometimes the solution needs to be kept at a particular temperature too.

- How much you dilute a disinfectant is important for it to work. If too strong a solution is used it may damage the surface. If it is too weak it may not work against the germs.

- Once diluted, disinfectants start to spoil. This means they lose their ability to work effectively against germs.

- It is important to keep clean the containers and equipment used in the dilution and for storage of disinfectants. Otherwise germs will grow in or on them, which will cause the disinfectant to become ineffective.

All cleaning agents must meet the Control of Substances Hazardous to Health Regulations (COSHH; see Health, safety and security, page 15).

- Remember the rules given on pages 117–19, Cleaning internal surfaces and areas.

TASK

What could go wrong if cleaning agents are not used correctly?

_____

_____

_____

Dealing with spillage of body fluids

Body fluids include blood, faeces, saliva, semen, urine and vomit. Such spillages must be cleaned immediately. This is because all body fluids should be treated as potentially infectious. Therefore, safe working practices must be followed at all times:

1. Cordon off the area and put out warning signs.

2. Wear a disposable plastic apron and gloves.

3. Identify the spillage. If you are not sure what it is, you must report it to your supervisor.

4. Get a spillage kit and follow the instructions on the label.

5. The spillage can be soaked up with paper towels. Put used paper towels in a clinical waste (see Dealing with routine and non-routine waste, page 105) bag.

6. Wash the area with a mop, detergent and water, and rinse several times with water and leave to dry.

7. Throw away your gloves and apron as clinical waste in a yellow bag.

8. Wash your hands carefully afterwards.

TASK

Describe the equipment and method you would use to remove the following spillages:

☐ Vomit on bed (plastic)

_____

_____

☐ Urine on altro floor

_____

_____

☐ Blood on walls

_____

_____

The correct order of work

The order in which you clean an area is important.

1 Assess the area to be cleaned including floors, walls, furniture fittings and waste containers, by looking at all the surfaces to be cleaned. These could be tiled walls, wooden furniture, ceramic fixtures and fittings, glazed surfaces such as windows, and soft, semi-hard and hard floors.

2 Then select the correct PPE. Prepare the area for cleaning by placing warning signs in a place where they can be seen. If necessary, cordon off the area.

3 Select the correct equipment for the soil type and surface to be cleaned. Make sure that the equipment you use is marked either by colour coding or otherwise for use in that area.

4 If there are spillages of bodily fluids on the floor, use a spillage kit or similar and follow the procedure for cleaning spillages. Remember that if you are not sure what a spillage or soil type is, you must ask your supervisor for advice.

5 Empty waste bins and check they are clean and remove any rubbish from the floor. Handle sharps and broken glass correctly, using a sharps box and gloves. The waste should be put into the appropriate waste container or appropriate coloured bag and labelled appropriately and taken to the internal or external collection points (see Dealing with routine and non-routine waste, page 95).

6 Then start cleaning the high surfaces with a damp cloth and the correct cleaning agent. Dry with a paper towel.

7 Now clean the surfaces etc. at eye level. Wipe over the bed frame, lockers and all fixtures and fittings with a clean damp cloth. Check underneath bed frame skirting boards, pipe work and corners and damp wipe. If there are any areas you cannot reach or cannot remove stains from, you must tell your supervisor.

8 Clean any glass surfaces and mirrors. If you need to remove any sticky items use a colour-coded abrasive pad. Polish with a dry cloth.

9 To clean soft floors use a vacuum cleaner starting in the far corner of the room and moving towards the door. Any stains need to be identified and treated with a cleaning agent according to the manufacturer's instructions.

10 To clean a hard floor use a vacuum cleaner if possible or a colour-coded dust control mop keeping the mop head in contact with the floor.

11 Using a colour-coded mop or a microfibre mop and bucket filled with hot clean water with added cleaning agent, clean around the edges of the room first (clean to dirty) using overlapping or figure-of-eight strokes of the mop. Make sure you rinse the

mop in the bucket frequently and do not use too much water. Change the water as it becomes dirty. Leave to dry or use a dry clean mop to help speed up the process.

12   Check that you have cleaned the room to a high standard. Remove your disposable apron and gloves and mask if used and dispose of in a clinical waste bag. Wash your hands before leaving the room.

13   Remove your cleaning equipment from the room. Dispose of the waste solution from the bucket down a sluice sink. Clean all the equipment. Check that the equipment is in good order and inform your supervisor if anything such as cleaning agents or consumables needs replacing.

14   Return all your equipment to the store room, ensuring that you lock the room after leaving.

15   If there is a washroom in the area, this should be cleaned first. Make sure you also clean door handles and wall switches, using colour-coded or labelled equipment.

Cleaning work schedules in hospitals

Wheelchairs and commodes should remain in the patient's room and be cleaned with a mild detergent and hot water followed by a chlorine based product after every bowel movement/patient's use. You will need to either change shoes or put on over shoes before entering a high risk area and wear disposable apron and gloves.

More frequent spillage of body fluids is likely, which means availability of spillage kits is essential, using 10,000 ppm hypochlorite granules or solution.

Contaminated linen needs correct disposal into the appropriate coloured linen bags inside the room, which are sealed and labelled. You must wear a mask and disposable gloves which should be removed and disposed of before leaving the room. Patients who are emotionally disturbed or distressed may require a nurse to be present while you are cleaning the room.

Equipment stored in the high risk area needs to be clearly marked that it is only to be used in that area. More frequent cleaning of door handles, light switches and door plates will be necessary. Use mild detergent and hot water or a detergent wipe followed by chlorine/hypochlorite solution containing product mixed to a concentration of 1000 parts to a million or use of a product such as Chlorclean. You also need to maintain a high standard of hand hygiene, washing your hands before leaving the room.

All cleaning should be done using separate colour-coded equipment and disposable cloths and ideally a colour-coded isolation precaution sign displayed on the outside of the door. Terminal cleaning will take place immediately after the discontinuation of isolation or barrier nursing. This involves the same procedure as above and in addition carpets steam cleaned. Curtains should be washed at the highest temperature suitable for the material. Any waste must be disposed of as clinical waste inside the patient's room.

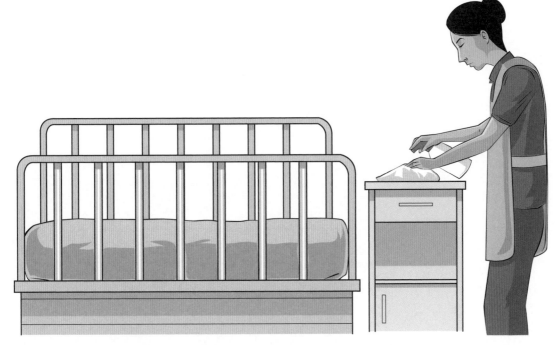

Figure 7.5. Cleaning tasks in hospitals are on going.

Cleaning work schedules in hospitals

TASK

From the areas listed below draw up a cleaning schedule for a hospital room that has:

A waste container	Walls	Hand wash basin
Bed frame	Floor	A glass partition

☐ 1. The order in which the areas should be cleaned

_____

_____

_____

☐ 2. The equipment and PPE required

_____

_____

_____

☐ 3. The cleaning methods to be used

_____

_____

_____

☐ 4. The cleaning chemicals or products needed

_____

_____

_____

☐ 5. Any additional considerations

_____

_____

_____

Refer to the NHS guidelines on cleaning work schedules in hospitals.

Cleaning work schedules in hospitals

TASK

 Describe how an acceptable standard of cleaning can be achieved in a hospital.

_____

_____

_____

TASK

 Why is it important to return the equipment and cleaning materials you have used to their original place?

_____

_____

TASK

 Give five examples of problems that may have occurred while cleaning that you should report to your supervisor.

1 _____

2 _____

3 _____

4 _____

5 _____

1 **When should you put on your PPE ?**

a. At home.

b. Before entering a high risk area.

c. Before the supervisor arrives.

d. When everyone else does.

2 **Why is it important to use different coloured equipment in high risk areas?**

a. So that you don't use too many mops.

b. So that you know which mop is yours.

c. So that the colour matches the walls.

d. So that the risk of spreading infection is reduced.

3 **Which of the following is a risk present in a high risk area?**

a. Tripping over a box.

b. Cross-contamination.

c. Feeling very cold.

d. Falling from a height.

4 **Before starting to clean a high risk area how would you let people know?**

a. Phone everyone.

b. Ask reception to tell everyone.

c. Display warning signs.

d. Assume that everyone already knows.

5 **How do you decide which is the correct cleaning agent to use?**

a. Ask another cleaner.

b. Use whatever is easiest to find.

c. Read the instructions on the products.

d. Smell it first.

6 **How do you know how much dilution to use for a floor cleaner?**

a. Ask a friend.

b. Guess and add a bit more for luck.

c. Read the instructions on the bottle.

d. Tell from the amount of foam.

7 **Why is it important to inform a supervisor if you are working alone in a high risk area?**

a. So that the supervisor can bring you something to drink.

b. So that the supervisor can arrange for you to have someone to talk to.

c. So that the supervisor can check that you are safe.

d. So that the supervisor will ask a colleague to help you.

8 **Why should you remove your jewellery before cleaning a high risk area?**

a. Someone might try to steal it.

b. It may get damaged.

c. It may spread infection.

d. You might lose it.

9 **When should you report an illness?**

a. When you have toothache.

b. When you have been sick.

c. When you are late for work.

d. When you see your supervisor.

10 **Which of the following PPE should you wear when cleaning a high risk area?**

a) Mask, goggles and knee pads.

b) Steel capped boots, knee pads and goggles.

c) Trainers, a baseball hat and gloves.

d) Gloves, apron, mask and goggles.

11 **What would you do if a piece of equipment you wanted to use did not work?**

a. Put it back in the store room and not tell anyone.

b. Tell a colleague.

c. Try another piece of equipment.

d. Tell the supervisor.

12 **Where is the best place to wash your hands?**

a. At home before you leave for work.

b. In the changing room.

c. Just before entering a high risk area.

d. Anywhere you can find a sink.

13 **When must you wash your hands?**

a. Before going out.

b. When you are told to.

c. Before entering and leaving a high risk area.

d. When everyone else does.

14 **Which of the following risks could be a cause of cross-contamination?**

a. An unknown spillage.

b. Using the same cleaning equipment for different areas.

c. Not washing hands properly.

d. All of the above.

15 **Why is it important to check with your supervisor before entering a high risk area?**

a. To find out if someone is going to help you.

b. To make sure you are wearing the appropriate PPE.

c. So that your supervisor knows you are working.

d. So that you can blame your supervisor if something goes wrong.

16 **With reference to cross-contamination, why is it important to report any item of damaged furniture or equipment to your supervisor?**

a. It makes the room look untidy.

b. The customer will be unhappy.

c. It could cause injury.

d. It could harbour germs.

17 **How would you identify a urine spillage?**

a. Ask another cleaner.

b. Guess.

c. Smell it.

d. Refer to your supervisor.

18 **What should you do with the warning signs when you have finished cleaning?**

a. Leave them out.

b. Clean them and put them away in the store room.

c. Put them away in a cupboard.

d. Leave them for the next cleaner to put away.

19 **What should you do with your uniform after finishing your cleaning in a high risk area?**

a. Leave it on and wash it at home.

b. Put it in the changing room for someone else to use.

c. Put it in a laundry bag.

d. Throw it away.

20 **How would you dispose of clinical/ hazardous waste?**

a. Put it in a yellow bag for collection.

b. Put it in a black bag for collection.

c. Wrap it carefully.

d. Disinfect it.

Chapter 8

Cleaning food areas

What you will learn:

- Food safety management
- Food hazards
- Sources of food hazards
- Pest control
- Importance of wearing PPE in food areas
- Personal hygiene practices
- Reporting health conditions
- Preparing the area for cleaning

- Cleaning equipment
- Cleaning agents
- Preparing the food production plant, equipment and materials for cleaning
- Cleaning the food production equipment
- Re-instating equipment in area after cleaning

Food safety management

The **Food Safety (General Food Hygiene) Regulations 1995** require all food businesses to have and follow a written set of food safety procedures (see Health, safety and security, page 3). These procedures are written by managers or supervisors, and are based on the **HACCP** (Hazard Analysis Critical Control Points) system. HACCP is a system that allows businesses to:

- identify **food hazards** within the business
- recognise the 'critical control points' (risks) in the process of food production at which food hazards may happen
- put in place procedures that will prevent or reduce the risk of food hazards
- make sure the procedures are working
- keep records of these procedures.

DEFINITIONS

Food hazard

A food hazard is something that could make food unsafe to eat.

HACCP

HACCP stands for 'Hazard Analysis Critical Control Points'. It is a system to identify and control possible food hazards.

Food Safety (General Food Hygiene) Regulations 1995

The Food Safety (General Food Hygiene) Regulations 1995 state the rules and regulations (see page 7) for the food industry.

Food safety management documents that you may use

You can obtain the documents explaining food safety management in your company from your cleaning supervisor.

Cleaning specifications

Cleaning specifications are a set of instructions for carrying out a cleaning task. These include:

- the area to be cleaned
- personal protective equipment (PPE; see Health, safety and security, page 8) required
- other equipment required

- cleaning products required

- cleaning methods to be used

- any special requirements, such as isolating any equipment from a power source

- any health and safety warning signs that should be used.

You should always have an up-to-date copy of the cleaning specifications before starting a cleaning task. This is because the instructions may have changed since the task was last carried out, for example a different cleaning product is to be used.

Risk assessments

A risk assessment identifies health and safety hazards, reviews the harm the hazard may cause and identifies actions to reduce the risk (see Health, safety and security, pages 4–6).

COSHH information sheet

COSHH stands for 'Control of Substances Hazardous to Health' (see Health, safety and security, page 15). This is a risk assessment carried out for chemical products. It provides information on the safe use of the chemical, any possible hazards and how it should be safely stored.

Product data sheets

Product data sheets (also called safety data sheets) are provided by the supplier of a cleaning product. This document is similar to a COSHH sheet, but it is specifically meant for a particular cleaning product. The product data sheet will include the recommended PPE and dilution ratios of the cleaning product (see Health, safety and security, pages 18–19).

TASK

Select one of the items from the list below to complete the following statement.

- A _____ gives instructions for completing a cleaning task.

  Risk assessment   Cleaning record   Equipment log   Cleaning specification

- A _____ gives all the required information about a cleaning product, including dilution ratios.

  Product data sheet   Friend   Cleaning record   Risk assessment

Food hazards

The law states that you have a responsibility to protect food, equipment and surfaces in the food area from contamination by food hazards such as bacteria, chemicals or physical objects. You also have a duty to understand what could happen if you do not follow them. This includes a risk to you.

All hazards should be reported immediately to the relevant person.

Bacteria or germs are present in food waste, raw food, on the skin of both people and animals and in their digestive systems, and in the air.

Cleaning products and chemicals used for pest control can be food hazards.

There are many objects that can fall into food, for example bits of string, parts from machinery, jewellery, food pest droppings, food pest egg cases or rubbish.

Sources of food hazards

The cleaner

Wearing dirty or incorrect PPE, insufficient or incorrect hand washing, health conditions including skin infections and diarrhoea are all sources of food hazards.

Personal items such as jewellery are also a hazard. Clothing could carry bacteria and you should remove and place items in a secure, clean and dry area away from food. This will prevent cross-contamination (see Health, safety and security-, pages 6–7).

Equipment

Dirty equipment, not following the correct colour-coding procedures, incorrect storage of cleaning equipment and equipment not assembled correctly are also sources of food hazards.

Cleaning products

Incorrect use of cleaning products, incorrect storage of cleaning products and not removing the cleaning product **residue** properly after cleaning could all contribute to contamination.

Waste

Incorrect disposal of waste after the cleaning task is also a risk.

Food pests

Pests are attracted to food premises, where there is warmth, shelter and possible sources of food. The contamination may come from their droppings, on or in their bodies and waste from their nesting area. The most common food pests are:

- insects: especially flies and cockroaches
- rodents: especially rats and mice
- birds: especially pigeons and sparrows.

DEFINITION

Residue

The remains of a substance on a surface are called residue.

TASK

Match each item to the food hazard it may carry by drawing arrows between them.

Container of de-scaler	Bacteria
A piece of jewellery (a ring)	Chemical hazard
Hands	Physical object

Signs of pest infestation

Signs of pest infestation are:

- sight of food pest – dead or alive
- droppings and nest sites
- gnaw marks on electrical cables .
- damage to packaging
- footprints in dust
- offensive smells
- greasy marks on walls around pipes (indicating route used by rats and mice).

Pests in a food area must be reported immediately as there is a possibility of foodstuffs, equipment and surfaces becoming contaminated. This contamination could cause somebody to become ill through food poisoning. This can result in legal action.

Chapter 8

Cleaning food areas

TASK

The presence of which pests may be indicated by each of the signs listed below? Choose from the list of food pests given at the bottom of the task. You may write down the name of a food pest more than once.

☐ Droppings

_____

☐ Sight – dead or alive

_____

☐ Nest sites

_____

☐ Damage

_____

☐ Any additional considerations

_____

| Rats | Dogs | Birds | Cockroaches | Cats | Mice | Flies |

Pest control

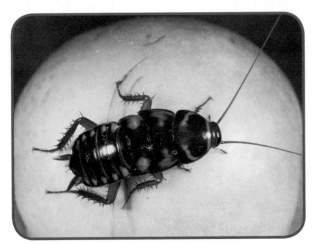

A cockroach nymph.

An adult cockroach.

Dealing with pest infestation

Your company will have carried out a risk assessment and have food safety management procedures in place for dealing with pest **infestation**. You should report signs of any pest infestation to your supervisor.

Most companies will have a contract with a pest control company. The pest control company will inspect the premises on a regular basis. It will monitor for the signs of pests as well as responding to any reports of pest infestation. The pest control operative may leave 'test baits' to attract any pests if they are present. This gives them an indication of the extent and type of pest infestation and helps them decide which method to use to destroy the pests.

> **DEFINITION**
>
> **Infestation**
>
> Infestation means that there are a large number of pests within a specific area and causing potential hazards to health.

TASK

Complete the sentence by choosing one of the people from the list below.

Pest infestations should be reported to a _____

Security guard   Cleaning supervisor   Close colleague   Maintenance worker

Cleaning areas of pest infestation

First you need to check with your supervisor if you have the authority to remove and clean an area of pest infestation.

The routine cleaning specifications may not include instructions on how to clear and clean an area of pest infestation.

However, you still have to follow correct procedures to prevent cross-contamination (see Health, safety and security, pages 6–7):

1 Wash hands correctly at appropriate times.

2 Wear the correct PPE.

3 Collect the correct cleaning products and colour-coded equipment.

4 Ventilate the area.

5 Place relevant signage in the area.

6 Remove loose debris (see Cleaning internal surfaces and areas, page 121) from the area.

7 Apply and remove the cleaning agents according to the manufacturer's instructions.

8 Ensure all surfaces are dry and free of residues.

9 Safely dispose of waste and **slurry**.

10 Check all cleaning equipment, cleaning products and PPE are clean, dry and securely stored.

DEFINITION

Slurry

Slurry is a dirty solution resulting from the cleaning process.

TASK

Number the steps in the correct order for preparing to clean a pest infestation area. The first step is numbered for you.

☐ Step ____: select and wear correct PPE.

☐ Step ____: collect cleaning equipment.

☐ Step ____: obtain cleaning specifications.

☐ Step __1__: check that you have the authority to clean the area.

Importance of wearing PPE in food areas

PPE is provided by your employer. You wear PPE in areas where unavoidable hazards still exist. PPE for cleaning in food areas includes:

- aprons

- gloves

- goggles

- masks

- footwear

- respirator.

PPE is meant not only to keep you safe but also to protect food and equipment from cross-contamination. Always wear the correct PPE and keep it clean and in good condition.

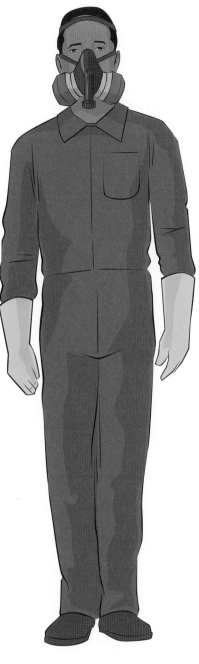

Figure 8.1. PPE prevents contamination.

Personal hygiene practices

According to the food safety regulations, you have a duty to maintain a high standard of personal hygiene (see Health, safety and security, page 10). This applies to anyone entering and working in food areas, including cleaning operatives. Good personal hygiene is also important for the professional image of your company and to give a good impression to customers.

If you follow the routines given below, you will minimise food hazards and possible contamination threats in your workplace:

- practise good hand hygiene
- wear clean and correct PPE
- report health conditions, such as open sores, diarrhoea and skin infections to your supervisor.

Essential hand hygiene

Always wash your hands:

- before starting work
- after visiting the toilet
- after coughing or sneezing into your hands
- after touching your hair or face
- before and after carrying out cleaning tasks
- when handling cleaning chemicals
- after handling dirty cleaning equipment
- after dealing with waste and waste containers
- before and after eating, drinking and smoking
- before re-entering a food area
- after changing gloves between cleaning tasks.

Personal hygiene practices

Wearing gloves for cleaning tasks is not a reason for not washing your hands.

To ensure your hands are washed properly you should always follow this process:

- always use a hand wash basin
- use hand hot water and ideally liquid antibacterial soap
- rinse hands thoroughly with clean water
- dry hands, preferably with disposable paper towels. Never dry hands on PPE, tea towels or clothing – you could cause cross-contamination.

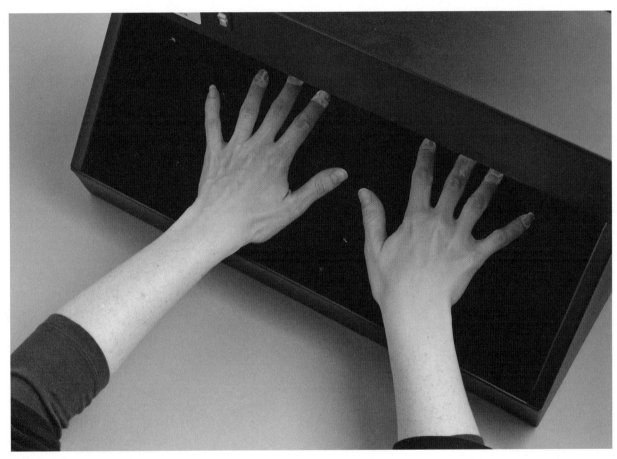

The ultra-violet light shows bacteria present on the hands.

Reporting health conditions

If you are ill you will be a food hazard yourself (see page 183). So if you have any of the following symptoms, you must report this immediately to your supervisor:

- diarrhoea
- discharges from ear, eye or nose
- vomiting
- septic wounds or cuts
- nausea
- open sores or skin infections.

TASK

Complete the sentence by choosing one of the people from the list below.

☐   Open sores and diarrhoea must be reported to a _____

Security guard   Cleaning supervisor   Company nurse   Production manager

Preparing the area for cleaning

Before you start cleaning, make sure that food and equipment is stored safely away from the cleaning area to prevent cross-contamination from cleaning chemicals and physical objects. It will also allow you access to clean the area and avoid wastage costs from **food spoilage**.

If you are cleaning a chilled or frozen food area, ensure that the food is stored in another chilled or frozen food area. This is to maintain the correct storage temperatures:

- frozen: at –18 degrees Celsius or below
- chilled: at 0 to 5 degrees Celsius.

The cleaning specification or your supervisor can give you advice on how to safely move and store food and equipment if you are unsure of what to do.

> **DEFINITION**
>
> **Food spoilage**
>
> Food spoilage is when food becomes unacceptable to eat, for example because of storing incorrectly or becoming contaminated with cleaning chemicals.

TASK

Complete the sentence by choosing one of the words from the list below.

- The most important reason to move food away from the cleaning area is to prevent _____ .

Waste   Contamination   Time   Theft

Colour coding

Equipment used in food areas is often colour coded. This means that one colour is designated for use in a specific area such as a food area. The main reason for using colour-coded equipment is to prevent cross-contamination. There is no nationally agreed colour-coding system for equipment. Your company may have its own or follow a system common to a group of companies. See also Cleaning high risk areas (page 164).

Cleaning equipment

The cleaning specification will provide guidance on the required cleaning equipment for a specific cleaning task. The cleaning equipment can be divided into two categories:

- Manual (small) cleaning equipment, e.g. colour-coded mops, cloths and buckets and scrubbing brushes.
- Electrical (large) cleaning equipment, e.g. scrubbing machines, pressure washers, steam cleaners, wet pick up.

There are some precautions you should take and health and safety checks that you should make before using cleaning equipment.

- Only use equipment that you have been trained to use.
- Check the equipment's PAT (portable appliance test) is up to date (see Health, safety and security, page 11) .
- Check the equipment is in good condition and clean.
- Check that leads and plugs are free from damage.

Any damaged equipment must be reported (according to your workplace procedures) to your supervisor, verbally or by completing the relevant documentation such as a **fault log**. You should also label the damaged equipment and if possible remove it to a secure place where it will not be used until it is safe to do so. This will prevent further equipment use and avoid any further damage to the equipment and the possibility of personal injury.

DEFINITION

Fault log

A fault log is a formal written procedure for reporting defective or damaged equipment and surfaces.

Cleaning food areas

Cleaning agents

Cleaning agents are the chemicals that are used to clean and treat different types of soiling and surfaces. It is important to select the most suitable cleaning agent to:

○ prevent damage, including permanently staining, discolouring or rusting to metal surfaces during cleaning

○ avoid the possibility of tainting food, e.g. using a disinfectant that has a strong smell

○ clean the surface effectively

○ clean the area within the allocated time

○ be cost-effective

○ prevent injury to yourself

○ avoid invalidating the manufacturer's warranty.

Besides chemicals, water applied under pressure will also work as a cleaning agent. Application of heat will kill some bacteria.

The cleaning specifications, product data sheets, manufacturer's instructions and COSHH sheets provide information and guidance about:

○ the suitability of the cleaning agent

○ the required PPE

○ the dilution rates

○ how to apply the agent, e.g. treatment times and suitable equipment

○ how to deal with an accidental spillage or ingestion of the cleaning agent.

> **DEFINITIONS**
>
> **Ingestion**
>
> Ingestion means eating or drinking something
>
> **Cost-effective**
>
> Economical use of time, equipment and cleaning chemicals is called being cost-effective.

Cleaning materials to be used when cleaning food areas

Alkaline cleaning materials are usually used for cleaning **organic matter**. **Acid cleaning materials** are used for cleaning **non-organic** matter.

The pH of a substance tells you how acidic or alkaline a substance is. This is important to know because the amount of acidity or alkalinity determines how effective the cleaning agent will be for a selected task.

The pH is represented by a number ranging from 0 to 14. Distilled water, which is pure water, has a pH of 7, which means it is neutral (that is, neither acidic nor alkaline).

In chemistry, pH 7 is the only neutral point on the pH scale. Anything with pH less than

7 is acidic and more than 7 is alkaline. But in terms of commercial products, materials with a pH of between 6 and 9 are considered neutral.

- Alkaline materials usually have a pH within the range 9 to 13.

- Caustic materials have a pH above 13 (although 'alkaline' is used to describe substances that have a pH higher than 7, caustic substances are those alkaline substances that will burn or destroy living tissue).

- Acidic materials usually have a pH within the range 0 to 5.

For a given product, the strength of the solution you make will affect its pH. For every complete point on the scale, the strength of the solution increases by 10. In other words, a product with a pH of 9 is ten times more alkaline than a product with a pH of 8.

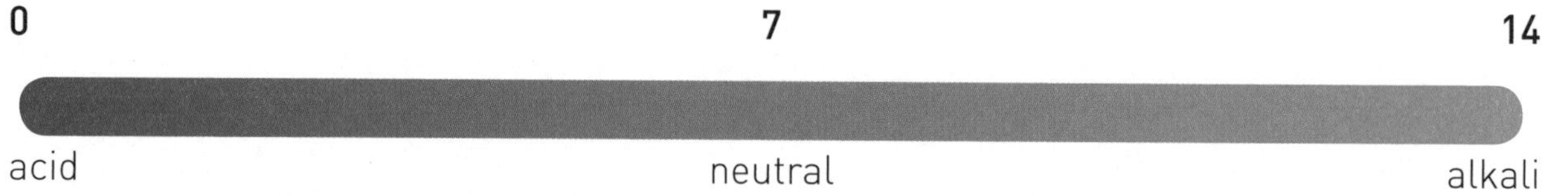

0   **7**   **14**

acid   neutral   alkali

Figure 8.2. The pH scale

To test whether a solution is acidic or alkaline you can use litmus or universal indicator paper. Follow the instructions supplied with the paper for doing the test correctly.

Chemicals should not be mixed. Chlorine and acid-based cleaners, such as toilet cleaners, will produce a dangerous gas if mixed. Mixing any acid cleaner with an alkaline cleaner will cause inactivation. This means they cancel each other out and become ineffective.

Neutral detergents

Neutral detergents (pH 6–9) are also called general-purpose detergents. As the name suggests these detergents are used for all routine cleaning. Approximately 80 per cent of micro-organisms can be removed from surfaces using a neutral detergent.

You should follow the manufacturers' instructions when using a neutral detergent. This is because if too much is used, the detergent may leave the surface sticky. A sticky surface is likely to retain or attract more dust.

Acid cleaners

The main materials used in the manufacture of acid cleaners are substances which are made from phosphoric acid, sodium bisulphate, oxalic acid, hydrochloric acid and sulphuric acid. Nitric acid can damage stainless steel if not diluted correctly. It is imperative that manufacturer's instructions are followed to avoid damaging surfaces.

Acid cleaners are usually diluted. You should measure the amounts carefully to avoid damaging the surfaces on which cleaners are used.

Acid cleaners are used mainly to remove non-organic material from surfaces, for example **limescale** from toilet bowls.

Alkaline detergents

Alkaline detergents are used for cleaning things that require a strong detergent to clean them. Examples are: hard surfaces, carbon black marks, a lot of dirt, very dirty walls and paintwork.

> **Hard surface cleaners** Hard surface cleaners usually have a pH of 9 to 11. They are used for cleaning surfaces with heavy soilage (see Cleaning and maintaining internal surfaces and areas, page 118), for example heavily impacted dirt or grease.

Glass cleaning products

Glass cleaning products are usually solutions made by dissolving chemicals in water. Some products have a very fine abrasive added to the solution.

Disinfectants

Usually you should not need to use chemical disinfectants for cleaning purposes.

The problems associated with using chemical disinfectants are:

- For **disinfection** to be effective, the surface first has to be cleaned to remove all traces of organic matter.

- No single disinfectant works against all the germs that could be present. So a variety of disinfectants are required to ensure surfaces are clear of germs.

- You need to leave a disinfectant in contact with the surface being cleaned for some time for it to be effective. This could be up to 30 minutes. During the contact time of the disinfectant the surface will need to be kept wet with the disinfectant solution. Sometimes the solution needs to be kept at a particular temperature too.

- How much you dilute a disinfectant is important for it to work. If too strong a solution is used it may damage the surface. If it is too weak it may not work against the germs.

- Once diluted, disinfectants start to spoil. This means they lose their ability to work effectively against germs.

- It is important to keep clean the containers and equipment used in the dilution and for storage of disinfectants. Otherwise germs will grow in or on them, which will cause the disinfectant to become ineffective.

Soil Types

Within a food area there is likely to be a variety of soil types, for example the soil left from pest infestations as already discussed in this chapter (see, pages 183–186). There are two particular types of soil associated with food areas:

- Polymerised: This is a greasy soil, which gives the appearance of a dried oil film. A hard water area presents a particular problem as the film bonds with the calcium in hard water and adheres itself in particular to floor surfaces. A variety of specialised cleaners are available for this particular type of soil.

- Carbonised: This is burnt or baked on food residue, which can often be difficult to remove.

Cleaning Agents

Alkaline stainless steel cleaners

After continual wipe downs, stainless steel equipment and surfaces can have a film on them and look dull. Using a stainless steel cleaning product, specially formulated for food areas will remove any residue left on the equipment or surfaces and leave it with a shiny finish.

Oven caustic materials

This is a highly toxic cleaning agent for using on burnt on residues. Specialist PPE and good ventilation is of the utmost importance when using this chemical.

Handling cleaning agents safely

A cleaning specification provides specialist information that is relevant to the equipment and area to be cleaned.

You will require a **permit** to enter certain food-related areas. Your supervisor may be able to obtain one for you. It is important that you check whether consent is required or has been obtained for you to enter and clean these areas.

An important health and safety task is for you to make sure any food plant or equipment is isolated (that is, disconnected from its power supply or the switch is switched off if it cannot be disconnected) before cleaning. So electrical plugs need to be pulled out and/or the main electrical switch turned off and gas supplies cut off.

Food production equipment, also known as in-place plant, is often not moveable because of its size or connection to power and utility supplies. It is most important that this equipment is isolated as described above, as often the equipment is directly connected to electrical supplies.

Appropriate warning signs must be in place to warn that cleaning is taking place and that the power supply should not be switched on. The warning signage used will follow workplace procedures and may range from placing a variety of signs to areas being cordoned off by tape or barriers. This is to prevent equipment being switched on and possible injury to you.

> **DEFINITION**
>
> **Permit**
>
> A permit gives you the consent or authorisation to be in an area, or to carry out a specific task.

Figure 8.3. Warning signs prevent equipment being turned on while cleaning is underway.

CAUTION

CLEANING IN PROGRESS

Chapter 8

Cleaning food areas

Preparing the food production plant, equipment and materials for cleaning

Before starting the cleaning task you will have:

- obtained a copy or checked the cleaning specification
- changed into the relevant PPE
- identified and collected the correct cleaning equipment and cleaning agents
- obtained permission to enter the area if required
- isolated the equipment and area
- put warning signs in place
- safely removed and appropriately stored any items, including food.

The next step to take is to take the food production equipment apart, also known as dis-assembly. This is vital to make sure that the equipment can be properly cleaned.

The equipment manufacturer's instructions will document the sequence that must be followed for dis-assembly and re-assembly. This is to prevent possible cross-contamination, prevent equipment damage, and to maintain the validity of any existing guarantee on the equipment.

The cleaning specification or your supervisor will provide the manufacturer's instructions. As well as manufacturer's recommendations for dis-assembly there may be workplace procedures for dis-assembly. This may include a designated area to hold equipment parts, which will help to ensure parts are:

- not mixed up
- not damaged or misplaced
- available in sequence for re-assembly
- not exposed to possible cross-contamination.

TASK

Number the steps in the correct order for preparing to clean a large piece of in-place food production equipment. The first step is numbered for you.

☐ Step ____: Make sure that the equipment's power supply is switched off.

☐ Step ____: Check appropriate warning signs are in place.

☐ Step ____: Remove equipment parts.

☐ Step _1_: Check that you have permission to clean the area.

Preparing the food production plant, equipment and materials for cleaning

It is essential to visually check and inspect all the parts of the food production plant at the start and during the dis-assembly process. Any damaged equipment must be reported immediately following your workplace procedures to your supervisor, verbally or by completing documentation, e.g. a fault log. You should also label the damaged equipment and, if possible, remove it to a secure place where it will not be used. This will prevent:

- further damage to the equipment
- the possibility of injury
- a likely food hazard
- any delay in equipment being repaired
- the cleaner being blamed for the damage.

Some food production equipment may only require minimal dis-assembly, for example shelving in an oven.

TASK

Circle the words or phrases below which are important for using a holding area for equipment components during cleaning.

Avoids losing machinery parts	Legislation limits
Contamination hazards	COSHH
Assists with re-assembly	Manufacturer's instructions
Prevents mixing up parts from different equipment	Minimises damage to parts

Cleaning the food production equipment

There is a wide variety of food production equipment, from a food service belt to deep fat fryers. Each has special cleaning requirements, which include:

- PPE

- cleaning equipment

- cleaning agents

- time allocated

- dis-assembly

- re-assembly.

However, you must always follow the general cleaning rules discussed earlier in this chapter. The special cleaning requirements noted above will be documented in the cleaning specifications. It is vital to follow the specifications as damage and personal injury may occur if the wrong cleaning equipment or cleaning agents are used. For example, harsh **scourers** on a metal surface may result in scratches and are likely to cause rusting.

To summarise, an organised logical approach to the cleaning task will maintain safe and effective working practices that include:

DEFINITION

Scourer

A scourer is an abrasive cleaning material, that is, it has a rough surface. Scourers should be used with care as they can scratch the surface.

- following cleaning specifications

- ongoing checking for equipment damage

- meeting timescales

- economical use of cleaning agents

- preventing accidents

- cleaning all equipment components

- preventing contamination hazards from poor cleaning, e.g. chemical residues not removed properly

- preventing damage to equipment or surfaces.

Re-instating equipment in area after cleaning

Like all procedures discussed in this chapter, you should follow an organised approach when re-assembling equipment and restoring the area after cleaning has been completed. The cleaning specification or your supervisor will provide the manufacturer's instructions.

The correct sequence for re-assembly is most important to prevent any damage to the equipment, cross-contamination and possible accidents. To prevent the possibility of these problems, you should:

- visually check for damage to equipment components
- visually check that all components and surfaces are free from cleaning agent residues
- report, following workplace procedures, damaged equipment, problems, including the cleaning specification not being met, to your supervisor, verbally or by completing documentation, e.g. a fault log
- after re-assembling, check equipment is in the correct working order
- return equipment and areas to their original position. This will also prevent complaints from the staff working within the food production area, as the work routine could be affected leading to loss of production and time being wasted
- check that equipment and surfaces are clean and dry.

TASK

Complete the sentence by choosing one of the people from the list below.

■ Problems identified during cleaning food production equipment must be reported immediately to the _____

| Security guard | Cleaning supervisor | Equipment manufacturer |
| Production manager | Facilities manager | |

Re-instating equipment in area after cleaning

After the final check of the equipment and area, the cleaning specification may require that some form of documentation is completed. This documentation may be kept as a record for the food safety management procedures of your company.

On completing cleaning you will probably have leftover cleaning agents, and there will be waste or slurry to dispose of. The disposal of these will depend on several factors including: environmental issues, type of chemical or waste and legislation (the law, rules and regulations).

A variety of guidance and information will be available to ensure the safe and legal disposal of these products. These include:

- cleaning specifications
- product data sheets
- manufacturer's instructions
- food safety management procedures.

Your supervisor should also be able to provide the information required.

Another task that you need to carry out is to clean and securely store the used PPE and cleaning equipment. This will ensure that equipment does not pose a contamination hazard when used again. It will also prolong the life of the equipment and will be readily available for the next person to use. Any damage to the PPE and equipment should be checked and reported.

Equipment storage areas should be:

- clean
- dry
- well organised
- secure
- well lit.

Knowledge test

1. **Which one of the following is the most important reason for having access to a food business's up-to-date cleaning specification?**

   a. To complete the cleaning task quickly.

   b. To satisfy workplace procedures.

   c. To check for any changes to the cleaning task.

   d. To check the area to be cleaned.

2. **Who is the best person to ask for a copy of the cleaning specification?**

   a. Your supervisor.

   b. A colleague.

   c. The security officer.

   d. Your customer.

3. **Which TWO of the following are the best actions to take to maintain a high level of personal hygiene when cleaning a food area?**

   a. Wash hands during the cleaning task.

   b. Change personal protective equipment.

   c. Read the product data sheet.

   d. Check the storage of cleaning agents.

4. **Which of the following is the most important reason for maintaining high levels of personal hygiene in a food area?**

   a. To prevent disciplinary action.

   b. To prevent equipment damage.

   c. To prevent cross-contamination.

   d. To prevent customer complaints.

5. **What is the most important reason to report health conditions?**

   a. To avoid infecting a colleague.

   b. To satisfy workplace procedures.

   c. To obtain replacement staff.

   d. To prevent cross-contaminating the food area.

6. **Who is the best person to report health conditions to?**

   a. Your customer.

   b. The receptionist.

   c. A colleague.

   d. Your supervisor.

7. **What is the best place to check the equipment required for a cleaning task?**

   a. The risk assessments.

   b. The cleaning specifications.

   c. The training records.

   d. The notice board.

8. **What is the best way to check equipment is safe to use?**

   a. Discuss the condition of equipment with a colleague.

   b. Visually inspect equipment for damage.

   c. Check the equipment's risk assessment.

   d. Read the equipment manufacturer's instructions.

9 **What are the TWO most important reasons for reporting faulty or damaged equipment?**

a. To prevent continued use of the equipment.

b. To prevent equipment being out of operation.

c. To prevent a delay in the equipment repair.

d. To prevent any possible accidents.

10 **What is the most important reason for isolating powered food production equipment before cleaning?**

a. To speed up the cleaning task.

b. To save gas or electricity.

c. To prevent accidents.

d. To meet the manufacturer's instructions.

11 **What is the most important reason for ventilating the cleaning area?**

a. To allow air circulation.

b. To stop any bad odours.

c. To disperse chemical smells.

d. To keep cleaning staff cool.

12 **Which TWO of the following documents are the most important in using safe and correct methods to clean food production equipment?**

a. Cleaning records.

b. Risk assessments.

c. Cleaning specifications.

d. Equipment log.

13 **What is the most important reason for maintaining the business's food safety management standards?**

a. To keep a good working environment.

b. To satisfy the customers.

c. To meet food safety legislation.

d. To maintain a good reputation.

14 **Which TWO of the following are common food pests?**

a. Rodents.

b. Dogs.

c. Cockroaches.

d. Reptiles.

15 **What is the most important reason to report signs of pest infestation?**

a. Avoid cross-contamination.

b. Prevent staff complaints.

c. Maintain a safe working area.

d. Keep customers satisfied.

16 **What are the TWO most important reasons to follow manufacturer's instructions for dis-assembly and re-assembly of food production equipment?**

a. To satisfy the cleaning specifications.

b. To avoid cross-contamination.

c. To identify machinery parts.

d. To prevent damage to the machinery.

17 **What are the TWO most important reasons for leaving the food area clean and hygienic after the cleaning task?**

a. To meet food safety legislation.

b. To prevent customer complaints.

c. To meet cleaning specifications.

d. To improve food production.

18 **What are the TWO main considerations when moving, storing and protecting food and equipment while cleaning a food area?**

a. To prevent food wastage.

b. To avoid possible cross-contamination.

c. To have easy access to food and equipment.

d. To ensure correct storage conditions.

19 **What are the TWO best places to find information about the safe and correct procedures for disposing of waste and slurry?**

a. Incident report forms.

b. Risk assessments.

c. Accident forms.

d. Produce data sheets.

20 **What is the most important reason to clean cleaning equipment after use?**

a. To avoid complaints from colleagues.

b. To prevent bad smells.

c. To meet workplace practices.

d. To ensure the equipment is ready for re-use.

Glossary

Acidic cleaning material: acidic solutions have a pH of less than 7.

Alkaline cleaning material: alkaline solutions have a pH of more than 7.

Ambient temperature: the temperature of the air around us.

Attitude: your opinions or views about something.

Bacteria: germs that are present everywhere, some of which can cause diseases in humans. Bacteria are very tiny, so they can only be seen under a microscope.

Body language: communication that takes place between people from the movements of their body and facial expressions.

Chemical disinfectant: [author to supply text at first proofs – please leave two lines]

Cleaning standards: the minimum acceptable level of work that a company wishes to provide for its customers.

Colour coding system: within a specified area different coloured equipment is used to carry out specific tasks.

Communication: the method of how we provide information to others.

Competent: a competent person is someone who is trained and qualified to identify existing and potential hazards. They also may have the authority to take action immediately if a safety hazard is identified.

Confidential: information that only certain people are allowed to access or read.

Consumables: any cleaning product that you use and have to replace from time to time.

Control measures: actions or procedures that are used to reduce health and safety risks while using certain products.

Cost-effective: in this context, the economical use of time, equipment and cleaning chemicals.

Cross-contamination: the pollution of one area with dirt or germs carried from another area or yourself.

Debris: dust and waste matter.

Demonstrating: showing someone how a task is done.

Dilution: reducing the strength of a fluid by adding water.

Disciplinary procedures: a formal process used by an employer to change an employee's behaviour or to ensure that the employee adheres to the employer's rules and/or policies.

Discrimination: treating or judging an individual or group differently from everyone else.

Disinfection: either reduces or destroys the ability of germs to grow. Disinfection can be carried out using chemicals called disinfectants, or sometimes just heat is used.

Diversity: valuing and embracing the differences in people.

Dust control mop: a piece of equipment that traps dust and prevents it re-circulating.

Efficient: being able to complete a task to a specific standard in a timely manner.

Emergency procedures: these tell you what to do if a potentially dangerous event such as a fire or a security alert occurs.

Enforcing authority: the enforcing authority is usually the environmental health department of a local authority.

Equality: the right of everyone to receive an equal level of respect and opportunity, despite their differences.

Fault log: a formal written procedure for reporting defective or damaged equipment and surfaces.

Feedback: a reply or response by the receiver to the sender of the original message. Feedback helps the sender confirm that the receiver has understood their message.

Food hazard: something that could make food unsafe to eat.

Food Safety Act 1990: states the rules and regulations for the food industry. It requires food to be treated in a controlled and managed way. The key requirements of the Act are that food must comply with food safety requirements, must be "of the nature, substance and quality demanded", and must be correctly described (labelled).

Food Safety (General Food Hygiene) Regulations 1995: cover general requirements for the design, construction and operation of food premises. The premises must be designed to allow food to be prepared safely with minimal risk of cross-contamination. The design must allow for adequate cleaning and/or disinfection. 'Dirty' work, such as washing/preparing raw food and washing up, should be carried out away from preparation of ready to eat foods.

Food spoilage: when food becomes unacceptable to eat, for example because of storing incorrectly or becoming contaminated with cleaning chemicals.

Gastro-enteritis: an infection of the stomach and intestines which can cause you to have diarrhoea (watery stools), and stomach pains. You may also feel sick and vomit.

Good practice: ways of working which not only meet the industry standards but improve on them.

HACCP: Hazard Analysis Critical Control Points – a system to identify and control possible food hazards.

Harassment: tormenting or bullying an individual or a group of people or making them worry about things unnecessarily.

Hazard: something that has the potential to cause harm.

Health and Safety Executive (HSE): the body responsible for ensuring that both employers and employees follow Health and Safety at Work laws and regulations.

Health surveillance: [author to supply text at first proofs – please leave two lines]

Industry standards: standards that are agreed throughout an industry as being the correct method or way of operating in that industry.

Infestation: pest infestation means that there are a large number of pests within a specific area and they are causing potential hazards to health.

Ingestion: eating or drinking something.

Job description: this is a list of tasks that you cover over a period of time.

Limescale: the white, chalky, hard material that collects where water resides, typically inside kettles or around taps and at the bottom of toilet bowls.

Memorandum: a note or a letter, but, unlike the newsletter, a memorandum is not sent to all the staff in a company. It is sent to some members of staff with information to help them with particular areas of their work.

Method statement: a method statement describes how to complete an individual task on the work schedule with a list of equipment and materials

Microfibre: a method of cleaning which does not require the use of cleaning products. The microfibres in the material act like a magnet and attract the dust, drawing it into the cloth.

Micro-organisms: germs that are too small for the human eye to see.

Newsletters: documents, either printed or electronic, written by different members of staff in a company and sent to all staff, containing news and information that everyone in the company needs to know.

Glossary

Non-organic matter: matter that comes from a non-living source, for example limescale, which is found in areas with hard water.

Organic matter: matter that comes from living or once living but now dead organisms. Examples include fingerprints, body waste, blood.

Permit: the consent or authorisation to be in an area, or to carry out a specific task.

Personal Protective Equipment (PPE): clothing that should be worn when there are risks to your own health and safety while working. For example, when working with chemicals or to avoid cross-contamination.

Pests: rats, mice and many insects, such as cockroaches and flies.

Personal hygiene: the way in which you look after yourself and make sure that you are clean and tidy.

PPE: *see Personal Protective Equipment*

Procedures: set ways of doing things. These are usually written down, either by a company or by a customer.

Recycling: the system of saving and processing used materials into new products in order to prevent waste of potentially useful materials. However, even if material is sent for recycling or undergoes treatment in-house, it can still be waste.

Regulations: rules that must be followed by law by all employers to avoid risks in the workplace that the government has identified. The rules describe the specific actions the government requires employers, and in some cases employees, to take to avoid risks.

Residue: the remains of a substance on a surface.

Resources: people, equipment and materials that are used to do a job.

Reviewing: looking back on your work performance and targets to check if you have achieved what you aimed for, assessing how you can complete your targets, and checking what you could have done better.

Risk assessment: a procedure by means of which the hazards present while doing a task are identified and the chances (risks) of that hazard occurring are estimated, taking into account any precautions that are already being taken.

Risk: the chance of a given loss occurring in specific circumstances.

Glossary

Safety management system: the formal process of assessing and making improvements to safety in the workplace and the tools used for work.

Sanitise: used in this context as a general term meaning the process by which a non-disinfected area becomes a disinfected one.

Scourer: an abrasive cleaning material, i.e. it has a rough surface. Scourers should be used with care as they can scratch surfaces.

Self-development: taking responsibility for your own learning and development.

Sharps: implements such as needles, syringes or blades that could pierce your skin or PPE potentially causing injury or passing on infection.

Slurry: a dirty solution resulting from the cleaning process.

Soilage: making something dirty or contaminated.

Static duster: The fibres in a static duster attract and hold the dust, preventing it from scattering and being re-circulated.

Staff handbook: a file of instructions on ways of doing things. A company usually wants all staff to follow its own handbook or set of rules.

Systems of work: procedures and practices put in place by employers to ensure that the health and safety of workers is not at risk while they are carrying out a function in an appropriate way.

Targets: set goals and ambitions that you aim to achieve within a given time period.

Ventilation: the process of letting air into an area to ensure a constant supply of fresh air.

Verbal communication: the passing on of information by directly speaking to someone, either in person or on the telephone.

Waste recycling: the collection, separation and clean up of those materials that can be reused.

Waste: 'Any substance or object which the holder discards or intends to, or is required to discard.' (The Environment Act 1995)

Work schedule: a list of jobs you need to complete on a given day. It usually has a timeline.

Written communication: the passing on of information by the written word.

Answers for Knowledge Tests

Chapter 1 – Health, Safety and Security

1. a	4. a	7. c	10. b	13. c	16. a	19. c
2. b	5. c	8. a	11. c	14. b	17. c	20. a
3. c	6. a	9. b	12. c	15. a	18. c	

Chapter 2 – Communication

1. d	4. d	7. d	10. a	13. b	16. c	19. a
2. d	5. d	8. d	11. d	14. c	17. a	20. d
3. b	6. b	9. c	12. d	15. d	18. d	

Chapter 3 – Working in teams and developing yourself

1. b	4. c	7. d	10. c	13. c	16. b	19. c
2. a	5. b	8. b	11. b	14. b	17. c	20. a
3. a	6. a	9. d	12. d	15. c	18. a	

Chapter 4 – Dealing with routine/non-routine waste

1. c	5. d	9. c	13. b	17. c	21. c	25. b
2. d	6. a	10. a	14. d	18. b	22. d	26. d
3. b	7. b	11. d	15. c	19. c	23. b	27. b
4. c	8. c	12. d	16. b	20. d	24. b	28. c

Chapter 5 – Cleaning of internal surfaces and areas

1. b,c	4. a,d	7. d	10. a,d	13. a,d	16. b,d	19. c
2. a,c	5. b,c,d	8. c,d	11. c,d	14. b	17. a	20. a
3. b,c	6. b,d	9. d	12. d	15. d	18. c	

Chapter 6 – Cleaning of washrooms

1. c	4. a	7. d	10. b	13. c	16. c	19. b
2. c	5. b	8. d	11. d	14. a	17. d	20. d
3. a	6. c	9. a	12. c	15. b	18. a	

Chapter 7 – Cleaning high risk areas

1. b	4. c	7. c	10. d	13. c	16. d	19. c
2. d	5. c	8. c	11. d	14. d	17. d	20. a
3. b	6. c	9. b	12. c	15. b	18. b	

Chapter 8 – Cleaning food premises

1. c	4. c	7. b	10. c	13. c	16. b+d	19. b+d
2. a	5. d	8. b	11. c	14. a+c	17. a+c	20. d
3. a+b	6. d	9. a+d	12. a+c	15. a	18. b+d	

Index

Index

rodents 97, 183

safe systems of work 6
safety data sheets 17–19
    examples 18–19
safety management system 2, 3
sanitary towel disposal 107
scourer 200
scrim 166
security procedures: premises 113
self-development 74–9
    see also developing yourself
semi-hard floors 125, 127
sharps 148, 165, 171
    disposal 105–6
skills
    showing others 65
    updating your 74–5
skips 100
slurry, disposal of 129, 186, 202
soft floors 125, 126, 171
spillages 90, 93, 100, 127–8
    body fluids 166, 170
    high risk 166
    known contaminant 144–5
    using disinfectant 144–5
staff handbook 39
standards, cleaning 71
static duster 122, 123
storeroom
    keeping tidy 114, 115, 129
    suspicious packages 8, 94, 113
switches and handles 172, 173
symbols on cleaning materials 23–6
systems of work 6

team 61–74
    answering questions 66
    asking for help 70
    communication in 33
    demonstrating jobs 65
    effective working 62
    feedback from 79
    handling disagreements 67–9
    joining discussions 73–4
    sharing knowledge 65
    supporting others 62
    welcoming new members 63–4
    what members need to know 64

telephone communication 35
    taking messages 35
terrorist attack, risk of 8
timesheets 52
toilet cleaners 150, 167
tyres, recycling of 87

urine spillages 170

vacuum cleaning 122, 125, 126, 171
    hospitals 171
ventilating area 121, 146, 147, 186, 196
viral disease 160
vomit spillages 170

warning signs 150, 151, 170
    on chemicals 23–6
    for hazards 23
    use of 121, 125, 197
washrooms 135–54
    cleaning materials 141–4, 150
    cleaning methods 150–1
    equipment for 140–4, 150
    handles and switches 172
    importance of cleaning 136–8
    key points 151
    knowledge test 152–4
    procedure 146–51
    reporting breakages 149
    waste products 148
waste 83–110
    clinical 101–102, 105–7, 170
    confidential 103
    disposal 95, 97, 101
    dry and wet 93
    and environment 84, 86
    food hazards from 182, 183
    hazardous 84, 86, 101, 166
    knowledge test 108–10
    methods for transferring 93–5
    mixed 104
    non-routine waste 86, 101–7
    PPE 90–1, 95, 100
    recording 96
    recycling 84, 87–9
    routine 86
    separation 166
    storage 84
    unidentifiable substances 103
    using wheeled containers 93–4
waste areas 100

waste collection points 95
waste containers 97–100
    keeping clean 99
    wheeled 93–4
Waste Management Licensing Regulation (1994) 105
Waste Transfer Notes 96
wet mopping equipment 127, 128
windows 171
Work at Height Regulations (2005) 21
work, safe systems of 6
work schedules 50, 114, 116, 121
Workplace (Health, Safety and Welfare) Regulations (1992) 21, 136
written communication 40, 41, 43–4

yellow waste bags 107